D1745917

Nesin Books, Inc.
İnönü Mahallesi Çimen Sokak No: 50/A Elmadağ Şişli/İstanbul - TURKEY
Tel: +90 0212 2914989 • Fax: +90 212 2341777
nesin@nesinyayinevi.com • www.nesinyayinevi.com

First published 2002
(Publishing Department of the Ministry of Culture of the Republic of Turkey)

Second edition November 2006
Third revised edition September 2009
Fourth revised edition May 2011
Published by Nesin Books
(Thanks to Elizabeth Ann Skewes and Çiçek Eriş for proofreading)

© 2006 Nesin Foundation and Nesin Books, Inc.
All rights reserved. No parts of this publication may be reproduced,
stored in a retrieval system or transmitted, in any form or by any
means, electronic, mechanical, photocopying, recording or otherwise,
without the permission of the copyright owners.

Executive editor
Atay Eriş

Cover design by
İlhan Bilge

001 02 01 001 - 55

ISBN 978-975-9038-83-0
Certificate No. 18231

Printing and binding by
Yazın Basın Yayın Matbaacılık Turizm Tic. Ltd. Şti. Çiftehavuzlar Cad. Prestij İş Merkezi No: 27/806
Zeytinburnu/İstanbul - TURKEY Tel: +90 212 5650122 Certificate No. 12028

Aziz Nesin

Laugh or Lament
Selected Short Stories of Aziz Nesin

Translated from Turkish by
Masud Akhtar Shaikh

Contents

7   Aziz Nesin - A Great Turkish Humorist
15 A Unique Surgical Operation
23 Our House and Our Landlord
28 Hang These Rascals
36 The Mother of Three Angels
41 I Committed Suicide
47 Precious Public Funds
55 What a Difference
62 Government Secrets Everywhere
66 The Shepherd and the Lamb
73 Freedom of Expression
81 The Ox Tells the Truth
88 Being Late For Work Competition
91 I am Sorry
97 A Stray Dog Named Tarzan
106 The Donkey and the National Service Medal
112 Agent 0X-13
121 Human Offspring
126 Chains and Shadows
135 The Cost of a Sensational Find
141 Corruption Unlimited
151 Beware of the Rats Amongst Us
155 The New Prime Minister

Aziz Nesin - A Great Turkish Humorist*

Aziz Nesin was one of the most famous modern writers of Turkey. Universally acknowledged as a master of satire, he has been adjudged by some critics as "the most forceful and prolific humour writer of this age". He was a poet, a novelist, a playwright, a journalist and a short story writer.

Although initially his name was carried into the international literary circles by some of his plays which were staged in Germany, America, and Romania, it is primarily his unsurpassed supremacy in the realm of short story writing that has established Aziz Nesin as a writer of global fame. He wrote over two thousand short stories, most of which have now been published in his books numbering more than ninety. Many of his books have been published in other languages, in Germany, France, Austria, Russia, Greece, Hungary, Bulgaria, Yugoslavia, Albania, Romania, Poland, Iran, and many of the Republics of the demised Soviet Union. One of his books, (The

---

* The writer of this preface and the translator of the book, Masud Akhtar Shaikh, was born in Rawalpindi (Pakistan) in 1928. After graduating from Gordon College, Rawalpindi in 1948 with Honours in English, he started studying journalism at the University of the Punjab at Lahore. He had an opportunity to study the Turkish language, both in Pakistan and Turkey. He qualified as a first class interpreter in Turkish language in 1963. He got deeply interested in Turkish literature. He translated a large number of Turkish short stories and poems into English, Urdu, and Punjabi. He undertook research work in Turkish, particularly its impact on Urdu and the regional languages of Pakistan.

Lunatic on the Roof) has been published in 23 different languages, including English, French, and Russian.

In his own country, most of his works have been published over and over again, the total number of copies having already exceeded the seven million mark, an achievement not yet equalled by any other Turkish writer. He was a four times winner of the first award in the International Humour Competition (Italy, 1956 and 1957, Bulgaria 1966, and Russia, 1969). He was also given the coveted LOTUS award by the Association of Afro-Asian Writers.

It has been a great privilege for me to have introduced this literary giant from a brotherly country, to the literary circles of Pakistan. My translations of his short stories have been appearing in Urdu, English, and Punjabi magazines and newspapers of repute since 1977. I have also published seventeen of Nesin's masterpieces in an Urdu book titled "Tamasha-e-Ehle Kerem". With a foreword by the late Faiz Ahmed Faiz, this book received a tremendous response from Pakistani readers and distinguished critics.

The Thorny Path to Fame

Aziz Nesin was born in a lower middle class family in Istanbul in 1915. Although intensely desiring to become a writer, his financial circumstances forced him to become an active soldier because in Turkey those days, the only way a poor boy could ever hope to become educated was to enter a military school. He graduated from the Army War School in 1937 and while still a soldier, started writing poetry. This was the beginning of his literary career.

He was dismissed from military service in 1944. In 1946, he was imprisoned for his writings. Before reaching the pinnacle of success as an author, the struggle for existence forced him to work as a grocer, a book seller, a photographer and even as a newspaper vendor.

By the year 1953, the government of the day had become so allergic to his name that newspapers were scared of publishing even an advertisement for a book carrying his name. His first book wasn't successful and ultimately he had to sell it by weight just to make part payment to the supplier who had agreed to provide paper for the book on credit.

From Nusret to Aziz Nesin

Originally named Nusret by his parents, this great humorist became Aziz Nesin through an amusing rigmarole of circumstances. When the Turkish government enacted a law requiring every Turk to adopt a family name, Nusret remained undecided about it till the last moment. In the meantime, he would ask himself in curiosity, "Nesin?" (Meaning: What are you? in a philosophical manner).

However, instead of becoming Nusret Nesin, he became Aziz Nesin (which should have been his father's new name). This also happened through a funny coincidence. In those days, senior officers hated to see writers in the army. To avoid their displeasure, Nusret used to write under the pen-name of Aziz which was actually his father's name. By the time he could use his own real name of Nusret Nesin without fear, he had become so popular as Aziz Nesin that it became a problem for his father to establish his own identity as the real Aziz Nesin!

When his father died, Nusret thought the problem had solved itself, little realising that another complication was to arise soon when he would start getting royalty for his publications in the name of Aziz Nesin, the deceased. It took him months to prove that it was in fact he himself, and not his father who had been writing as Aziz Nesin.

The Comedy of Cover Names

Talking of names, Aziz was not the only cover name that this great writer employed. He touches upon this subject while explaining his remarkable success as a poet during his early career:

"The reason for my popularity was not the beauty of my poems but the fact that these used to appear under a feminine cover name. This female cover name brought to me loads and loads of love letters showering glorious tributes on me and my poetry."

Right from the very start, his writings used to attract the wrath of the government of the day. Consequently, the press was always reluctant to publish anything bearing his name. It was then that he resorted to the generous use of cover names. As soon as a publisher realised that the real author behind a cover name was Aziz Nesin, he would refuse to accept any more material under that name. But Aziz would outwit the publishers by switching over to a fresh nom de plume. Thus, by having written under more than two hundred cover names, he has become a unique writer in the history of literature.

The use of cover names sometimes resulted in highly interesting and at times extremely embarrassing situations. One of his stories was published under a French cover name. It later found its way into the "Anthology of World

Humour," as a typical example of French wit. Another story of his was published under a Chinese cover name and later reappeared in a certain magazine as a translation from the original Chinese!

When Nesin was first arrested for his writings in 1946, the police kept him under pressure for a whole week to disclose the actual identity of the person whose writings had been appearing under the name 'Aziz Nesin.' They did not believe that the writer was in fact Nesin himself. Two years later, exactly the opposite happened. This time, the police insisted that Nesin was the actual author of some objectionable writings that had appeared under some other name. And this time he really was not the author of those writings! One such incident resulted in his imprisonment for sixteen months when the legal experts succeeded in proving to the court that an objectionable article had been written by him whereas in actual fact he was not its author.

It was only after 1956 when Nesin won the first Gold Palm Award for Humour in Italy that the Turkish press started accepting his writings under his real name. That was when he could finally dispense with the use of cover names as a writer.

Poet Turned Humorous Story Writer

"Right from my childhood," writes Nesin, "I had wanted to write tragic stories that could draw tears from the readers' eyes. I took one such story to a magazine. The chief editor went through the manuscript but, being a man of little understanding, he burst into laughter instead of shedding tears as I had expected any sensible reader to do. His eyes did become wet, but with tears of laughter.

At last he said to me: 'Well done! Very good. Write some more stories of this type for us.' That disappointment in my early career as a writer has continued till today. The stories that I write primarily to make my readers cry, make most of them laugh".

Nesin's writings do make the readers laugh, but they contain immense food for thought for those who care to read his message, which is enshrined in light, satirical language. He writes with a purpose and the purpose is to champion the cause of freedom of the press from all artificial curbs, freedom from fear, want, hunger, disease, ignorance, and unhealthy social customs, freedom from the shackles of officialdom and red tapism that make the life of the common man miserable. He particularly excels in the field of political satire. His targets are the politicians and the political parties, whether in power or in the opposition. He flays them ruthlessly for their false promises before elections and for their unbridled exploitation of the masses.

Just as a highly skilled surgeon uses his lancet to reach the most intricate regions of human body in order to locate and eliminate its diseased portions, so does Aziz Nesin use his pen in a desperate bid to rid society of its common maladies - corruption, worshipping the rising sun, flattery, double standards, back biting, selfishness, immorality, trading in human flesh, smuggling, black marketing, etc.

While highlighting various social evils, Nesin does not make his characters an object of our hatred; instead, he rouses our sympathies towards them and convinces the readers of the need to reform these unfortunate victims of social injustice through a collective effort by the whole society. He is a close friend of the poor and the under-dog, the tillers of the soil, the petty shopkeepers, the low-paid employees, the teachers, and, above all, the child. He vehemently supports the child against the vagaries of the grown-ups and has a particularly soft corner for the class of unfortunate children called orphans.

A Great Philanthropist

The man who, as a dismissed army officer, with a reputation of being a versatile writer, was compelled by circumstances to become a newspaper vendor to be able to feed his children, became a millionaire a couple of decades before his death. However, he set aside his millions for the children of others, not only for his own kids. He became one of the biggest philanthropists of Turkey. The entire income from his books was allocated by him for all times to come, for financing the Nesin Foundation. The Foundation was given the noble aim of protecting children from the miseries and deprivations from which Nesin himself had been suffering when he was a child. This perpetual legacy of Aziz Nesin accepts a few orphan children every year and provides them free education from primary to the university level, with free residential facilities, food, clothing, and other necessities of life. Although Nesin died in 1995 at the age of 80, Nesin Foundation continues to serve as a beacon of light for those whose hearts bleed for the sufferings of others and who want to contribute their time and effort for the alleviation of human misery.

A Unique Surgical Operation

The importance of the 10th International Surgical Congress could be gauged from the extraordinarily large number of delegates participating in it and the very high standard of papers read during its various sessions. The delegates were all surgeons of international fame. Journalists representing major news agencies of the world had come to cover the proceedings, although the news value of a surgical congress does not normally match that of a film star's press conference or even a fashion show. Prominent doctors from twenty-three countries had formally notified their intention to read papers on various subjects. Amongst them were surgeons who could strip and reassemble every part of the human body with the adroitness of a watchmaker who can handle hundreds of tiny components of a watch.

Inaugural ceremonies took the best part of the first day of the congress. The next day was devoted to papers of a general nature. The most anxiously awaited was the third day which had been set aside for special professional presentations. The first delegate to appear on the stage that day was Dr. C. Claseman, a renowned American surgeon. He was accompanied by another gentleman. The audience had donned their special head phones and were waiting impatiently to hear Dr. C. Claseman. Arrangements had been made for simultaneous translation of all speeches into four major world languages, and the audience could listen to the language of their choice by pressing the appropriate button. Pressmen were all ears, their papers and pens at the ready. At last Dr. C. Claseman commenced his dissertation:

"Ladies and gentlemen! I have performed innumerable operations during my thirty-five years career as a surgeon. This morning I shall talk to you about the most interesting and unusual operation of my life. As you are all aware, no surgeon in the world has so far succeeded in changing an individual's finger-prints. Even if the original skin of a person's fingers is removed, the skin growing anew bears exactly the same finger-prints. No matter how often you may remove the skin, every time it will reappear with the same original pattern of lines. This peculiar characteristic is made use of by the police in identifying and arresting thieves, robbers, murderers and other criminals.

"It gives me great pleasure to announce that I have long been in possession of a technique that enables me to completely change a person's finger-prints. The gentleman you see with me on the stage is Mr. Thomas, a well-known business magnate of our country. He is also called Jack the Jawbreaker. This is the name by which he is known in the old records of FBI. He is desperately wanted by the FBI in connection with numerous bank robberies involving millions of dollars. My new surgical technique has frustrated all its endeavours to apprehend Mr. Thomas aka Jack the Jawbreaker because, after every robbery that he commits, I change the pattern of Mr. Thomas' finger-prints. I have found no other surgical operation to be financially as profitable as this one. And why shouldn't it be, when the doctor shares the spoils with his robber patient on fifty-fifty basis! Now, with the help of a film and some slides, I shall demonstrate to you how I conduct this operation."

After Dr. C. Claseman had demonstrated his novel technique, there was a general consensus of opinion amongst the audience that he was going to be declared the most successful surgeon of the world. However, their opinion was soon changed when Mr. B. Leanes, a British surgeon, appeared on the stage and described his own startling achievement. He too was accompanied by a gentleman. Mr. B. Leanes began his address thus:

"Honourable friends! I shall discuss with you the details of what may easily rank as the most remarkable operation ever conducted on the battle-field. Sergeant Mattew, whom you see with me on the stage this morning, is a very brave soldier. During the Second World War, he fought single-handed against twenty-six enemy soldiers and wiped out every one of them. Unfortunately, he was hit by an enemy mine and was decapitated. I operated upon him and with the help of a special surgical compound which I had invented, I managed to replant Mr. Mattew's severed head on his body. The same head now stands so firmly fixed on his neck that, let alone a mine, even an atom bomb could dislodge it. I shall now explain the formula of this miracle compound which I use for bonding human organs."

Spell-bound, the audience listened to Dr. B. Leanes' explanation and observed his demonstration of a revolutionary technique in surgery. They were unanimous in their view that no surgeon had ever performed a more interesting and startling operation in the history of surgery. Nevertheless, this opinion was also changed pretty soon when a French doctor took the rostrum. Unlike the two previous speakers who were helped by male companions, the French doctor was accompanied by a beautiful damsel, dressed in a bikini, as if ready for a beauty contest. Her appearance on the stage caused a stir amongst the audience. The doctor introduced his subject with the following words:

"My dear colleagues, ladies and gentlemen! I am going to talk to you about an operation conducted by me involving plastic surgery. I am thoroughly convinced that no other surgeon has ever been able to perform such a unique operation as this. I am sure all of you will readily agree with me in classifying the operation as the most outstanding achievement of surgery when I tell you that the beautiful young girl whose appearance on the stage a few minutes ago caused many a heart to flutter, is none other than my sixty-five year old mother-in-law."

Then he narrated how his own wife had betrayed him by eloping with somebody else, and how merely to wreak vengeance on his former wife, he had decided to turn her widowed mother into a young girl through plastic surgery. In a highly learned and elaborate discourse, he enlightened the audience about the manner in which that most outstanding of operations had been performed by him.

Every paper read during the Congress described an achievement in the field of surgery that excelled all others in uniqueness and pre-eminence. This is how the German surgeon rightfully boasted of his own singular performance:

"Distinguished delegates! You know when a person dies, all his organs do not become lifeless at the same time. For instance, if a person dies of a heart attack, it would be normal to find all parts of his body except his heart, to be in perfect state of health at the instant he breathes his last. Similarly, one dying of tuberculosis has only a pair of diseased lungs while the rest of his body still has its normal life-span to complete. For many years I kept pondering over this phenomenon, wondering how the death of single organs could result in the complete incapacitation of a whole range of human organs which are collectively much bigger than the decayed component. My inquisitiveness led me to a stage where the collection and preservation of various living parts from the bodies of dead patients became a virtual mania with me. Ultimately, I succeeded in assembling these retrieved parts into a full-fledged human being. And the result you can see right in front of you on the stage. This man here is the product of my efforts."

Pointing towards his colossal companion, the doctor continued.

"His legs belong to a sportsman who died of kidney failure; his torso belongs to a wrestler whose death was caused by a gangrenous leg; his skull belongs to a man who left this world as a result of tuberculosis."

Who could ever imagine somebody collecting the surviving organs of dead bodies and converting them into normal human beings pulsating with life? This was just like a carpenter fabricating a piece of furniture to meet a customer's demand.

The German surgeon Dr. Günther would have been voted as the most successful surgeon of the world, had it not been for the Japanese delegate who disclosed a still more remarkable achievement at the next morning's session of the Congress. The Japanese surgeon Himi Shiyama was also accompanied on the stage by a companion. He began with the following words:

"Honourable fellow surgeons! This friend of ours whom you see with me this morning was born lame and therefore was refused enlistment in the army during World War II. This was a grave insult for any Japanese. So he decided to commit suicide through hara-kiri. The moment he poked the sharp-edged knife into his abdomen, his bowels littered with blood, gushed out and dropped on the road. I managed..."

It was the last day of the 10th International Surgical Congress. Presentation of papers had come to an end. Suddenly, the Chairman of the Congress noticed a delegate who had been sitting quietly in a corner of the hall throughout the proceedings and had not read any paper.

"Wouldn't you like to contribute to the proceedings of this Congress, doctor?" enquired the Chairman. "We would certainly like to benefit from your valuable professional experience as a surgeon."

"Mr. Chairman," replied the doctor, "I have a long professional career and a large number of operations to my credit, but I don't consider any of these to be of such an extraordinary nature as to merit presentation to this august body."

Thinking that the honourable delegate was being unpretentious, everybody pressed him to come out with his most outstanding experience for the benefit of the entire community of world surgeons. The doctor went forth to address the Congress:

"Gentlemen! Since you all insist, let me tell you about a small operation which I recently performed in my own country. It involved the removal of a patient's tonsils."

This aroused a hearty laughter from all those present. Their ridicule was understandable. Wasn't it silly on the part of the worthy doctor to talk of such an insignificant operation as the removal of tonsils, in the presence of scores of giants from the world of surgery? And that too after the singular achievements of others had left the whole world spell-bound for the last so many days!

Offended by ridicule, the speaker tried to defend himself:

"My dear friends, may I tell you that I was just trying to be humble when I said I had no extraordinary operations to my credit. The fact of the case is that the tonsils operation I was going to describe to you was by no means an ordinary operation."

These remarks made the audience laugh longer and louder. Somebody from amongst them interjected:

"He thinks removing tonsils is surgery!"

"I make my nursing assistants do that," retorted another.

"Rather than bragging about it, a surgeon should be ashamed of talking about tonsils at this level," shouted still another delegate.

The speaker was infuriated by what he considered to be the uncalled for remarks of the audience. He again pleaded his case:

"Do you know who the person was whose tonsils I removed?"

"Be he the secretary general of the United Nations!" replied a delegate. Will that make any difference? A tonsils operation is just a tonsils operation no matter who the patient may be."

"Worthy friends! Let me tell you that my patient was a journalist," shouted the annoyed speaker. The audience roared with laughter. Then someone remarked:

"A journalist or a trader, a high ranking official or a humble soldier, everybody's tonsils are the same as far as surgery is concerned."

"You are very right sir," conceded the speaker, "but you may like to know that when I performed the said operation, there was absolutely no freedom of press in our country. Accordingly, journalists were not allowed to open their mouth at all. As my patient happened to be a journalist, I had no alternative but to approach his diseased tonsils through an opening other than his gagged mouth."

The guffaws of the audience froze on their very faces. Their ridicule immediately turned into applause and appreciation. The unanimous verdict of the meeting was that, of all the surgical achievements disclosed by eminent world surgeons during the 10th International Surgical Congress, the most unique, difficult and unmatched was the one dealing with the removal of a journalist's tonsils when the press laws of the country did not allow the patient to open his mouth.

Our House and Our Landlord

I live in a seven storey apartment. It has five storeys aboveground and its two storeys underground are like a mine. Actually, below these underground storeys there is another half a storey in which I reside. I have been living here for two years but have not yet been able to determine whether the ceiling of our apartment is lower than the lowly landlord or vice versa. But the fact remains that in spite of my short stature, the ceiling hanging above us like the Sword of Damocles hits my head twice or three times a day, warning me to be careful next time.

I am quite happy with this house for a number of reasons. For one, it has no great scenic beauty about it. This keeps reducing our appetite, gradually helping us make both ends meet within our legitimate income without risking our self-respect.

Again, since air can by no means enter the house, we don't run the risk of catching cold or flu. Not only the air, not even the sun can make an inroad into our rooms. This saves our curtains from fading. You may say the sun is ignorant of our address. Well, the sun may be, but the tax authorities and their staff certainly are not, for they reach us as easily as if it is they themselves who had planted this building where it stands today.

Another advantage of this house is that, being underground, it defies all attempts of those who take pleasure in secretly watching others in their privacy. A determined secret watcher will have to equip himself with a periscope, like a submariner, and even then he will be getting nothing but shame, for there is hardly anything in this house worth watching secretly, thanks to our meager pocket.

You keep count of the blessings of this house and still these won't come to an end. The water, for instance. There is absolutely no question of any water shortage here. The water supply of the whole of Istanbul may be disrupted and the entire population may be grumbling of parched tongues but water would be aplenty in our house. Take a tap and insert it at any random point in any of the walls and then turn on the tap. And lo and behold! Water starts gushing out. Often you don't have to take even that much of trouble, for our kitchen has some big pits in its floor from which you can fill a bucket any time, using an ordinary mug.

The previous tenant of this house was a canny man. He could not put up with the misery of the Istanbullites due to the perpetual water scarcity, especially during the sizzling heat of summer. He installed long rows of taps in the walls and started filling bottle after bottle of water for sale under the brand name "Wall Spring Water". One could see long queues of water carriers outside this house as if it was some sacred spring with healing qualities. Healing qualities it did have. Those who consumed two bottles of this water were sure to have their stomachs, intestines and what not, thoroughly cleansed.

However, because of certain side effects of over-dosage, it was soon made mandatory for the prospective buyers to produce a doctor's prescription. It was proved that those who drank ten bottles could get rid of the stones in their kidneys as well as those stuck in their bladders. However, they ran the sure risk of losing not only their very kidneys and bladders but also their intestines into the bargain. Prolonged use over a period could turn human beings into statues because of the very large deposit of lime in their whole system, starting from the mouth right up to the point where intestines terminate.

The greedy landlord who had seen that the previous tenant earned money from the leaking water, managed to obtain an unfitness certificate from the municipal medical authority and thus had the house vacated. It was then that it was rented out to me. The landlord had become wiser this time. So he got a new clause inserted in the contract, depriving me of the right to draw the seepage water from the walls for commercial use. Of course we were allowed to use it for own consumption. We were soon to be compensated for this loss of privilege.

We noticed that the walls of the corridors had a thick layer of saltpeter due to humidity. We scraped it and collected a substantial quantity. Being a precious commodity, it fetched us a good amount when we sold it to the tinsmith. We have been repeating this process because the walls keep turning out saltpeter regularly. We do this secretly for fear of being ejected by the greedy landlord.

The day the month starts, we find our landlord standing at the door. This he does with the immaculate regularity of a metronome. As a matter of fact, it is his visit that reminds us of the beginning of a new month. If you request for the deferment of payment of rent for a couple of days, he starts entreating and pleading for immediate payment in such a pathetic manner that one feels to pay him not only the rent but also to obtain a bank loan on heavy interest in order to give him. The poor fellow has to pay loan installments and bills amounting to thousands of Liras every month. And he seldom forgets to carry all these bills on his person so that he could easily convince you of his compulsions.

Another characteristic of our house is that you find here all known and unknown types of insects like ants, cockroaches, centipedes, bugs, gnats, flies and mosquitoes. They say a previous tenant, a German professor of Zoology at the Istanbul University, had discovered in this house three species of insects which had till then not been known to the world of science. While returning to his country, he carried with him the world's richest collection of insects from this place. This was told to us by our landlord in support of his refusal to reduce the rent. According to him, the German professor used to say:

"It's a pity you people don't know the true worth of your treasures. If we ever had such a place in Germany, we would immediately turn it into a zoological garden-cum-museum. There would then be no need to send your kids to school. They could see and learn everything about every living thing at that very place."

Originally, our landlord used to be the door-keeper of this very building. Starting with the ownership of a door, he became the owner of this whole edifice.

I remember once I could not pay him the rent on due date. He lost no time coming to the office of the magazine where I work. Twenty years earlier he had also been the doorman of the owner of our magazine. He immediately recognised our landlord and enquired:

"Hello Ali, Sir! What brings you here?"

"I've come to realise the rent, Sir."

"How's that? Don't tell me you have an apartment of your own by now."

Our landlord did not relish these remarks. He protested:

"Be fair. Sir. I have been measuring the footpaths of Istanbul for full 22 years. Even now you grudge me an apartment?"

Having been born and brought up in Istanbul and having lived here in rented houses, not for a mere 22 years but for full 42 years, I felt a sense of shame. The landlord had not told my boss that it was not just one apartment that he owned. In addition to that, he had managed to buy another one, plus a house in Nishantashi, a few plots here and there, and a shop on top of all these.

But what use were all these to him when shortly after this incident, he was caught red-handed while indulging in black marketing on a large scale. He was sent to jail by the Controller of Prices. As the man had done us some good turns, we went to see him in the prison. I took with me a few packets of second class cigarettes for him. I saw him shedding tears behind the bars. I tried to console him:

"Don't grieve, Ali, Sir. You have been in Istanbul for full 22 years but never been inside its jail. Now that you have seen the way to it, you will keep coming here and will soon get used to it."

Hang These Rascals

Istefano was a habitual criminal of the town, with over a hundred crimes to his credit. In police records he was known as "Technical Thief". He had earned his title on account of his weakness for stealing electromedical instruments. He had specialised in the art of clinic-breaking in preference to house-breaking. His reasons were quite logical. Firstly, clinics are easier and safer targets than residences, there being no inhabitants, no servants, and no watch-dogs at night. Secondly, it was comparatively easier to dispose of the stolen stuff.

In his tricky profession, Istefano was assisted by Freckled Tekin who had at first joined as an apprentice but had reached the covetous status of an aide-cum-confidant through his constant loyalty and sheer hard work over the years.

The time was past midnight. Istefano and Freckled Tekin reached their target area. As usual, they had reconnoitered the surroundings during the day and had drawn up a plan of action. The massive Great Effort Building housing a number of clinics, had no security lights. The two went to the rear of the building. Freckled Tekin positioned himself behind a tree, ready to send forth a pre-fixed warning signal to his "Guru" at the slightest indication of danger. Istefano climbed up a sewerage pipe with the dexterity of a monkey, and was soon standing in the balcony of the first floor. With the help of a high-efficiency glass cutter, he made a neat hole in the large window pane. A little glue applied to his left hand prevented the broken glass piece from falling on the ground. Inserting his arm through the gaping hole in the pane, he opened the window that had been bolted from inside. Before going in, he whistled to Freckled Tekin to ascertain if it was all clear. Freckled Tekin responded with the "go-ahead" signal. Istefano went in. He scanned the room with a torch, picked up an electro cardiogram, and within a few minutes rejoined his deputy down below.

Later the same night, Istefano and Freckled Tekin repeated their performance in another clinic in Labour Apartment. By faithfully adhering to their standard drill, they had achieved their limited objective for that night, viz, two electro-cardiograms, without burning their fingers.

On the main entrance to Great Effort Building, you could see a large, shining name plate in thick brass letters. It read: "Dr. Orhan, MBBS, MRCP, Heart Specialist." Dr. Orhan had been terribly upset during the past one week. Someone had broken into his clinic and decamped with his precious electro-cardiogram. For the whole week, day in day out, he had been narrating this catastrophe to all his friends and acquaintances. By now he had memorised every single word of his tale of woe. The way he disgorged the story reminded you of a theatre artist who performs the same role night after night for weeks, in the process learning by heart every word of his dialogues without any conscious effort on his part.

The refrain of Dr. Orhan's story went something like this:

"By God, I am in a terrible fix these days. Do you know somebody has pinched my electro cardiogram? I left it intact in the clinic at night but it was missing next morning. The thief entered from the rear balcony. The police say they are trying to trace the culprit but you know the way our police works. While they are still busy with their usual formalities, I continue to suffer for lack of this vital instrument. It had cost me full ten thousand liras. But it's not the money that matters, you know. Money one can earn as long as one lives. The trouble is that the wretched thing is unfortunately not available in the market at any price. The government banned its import long ago. They thought it was an unnecessary drain on our foreign exchange earnings. How silly! You can't get it in the black market either; otherwise I don't mind paying even twenty thousand to get it. I am feeling like a man who has been deprived of his two hands, a feeling of sheer helplessness, you know. Just imagine the financial loss I have been suffering since this incident. By a very conservative estimate, I see twenty patients daily. Multiply this figure with the very nominal amount of fifty liras that I charge every patient, and you'll get a figure of a thousand liras a day. A net loss of thirty thousand a month!

"You may ask me why a burglar should lay his hand on an electro cardiogram. Yes, that's a million dollar question. The man in the street has absolutely no use for it. I am sure the gadget is going to find its way to the clinic of another doctor, a fellow member of our fraternity. Now you tell me, won't that worthy gentleman belonging to this so-called noble profession of ours be fully aware of the fact that the instrument he is going to buy is the stolen property of a brother doctor, that the seller is definitely a thief? If so, why should he patronise a thief? He will patronise him because he is goaded purely by selfish motives, bothering the least about the ethical code of conduct by which he swears morning, noon, and midnight. He will get the thing dirt cheap from that vagabond, paying a couple of thousand liras for an item that would otherwise cost him a fortune these days. Then why should he be interested in ethics, and why should his conscience prick? The conscience of that rogue of a doctor must be dead in any case, otherwise he would immediately hand over the thief and the stolen gadget to the police. If you ask me the real burglar is not the man who has committed the theft; it is the sucker who is going to buy it. They call themselves doctors, but in fact they are the scum of our profession. Why should we blame the thief? He steals because that is his vocation.

"But look at the parasites who foster burglars by buying stolen stuff from them. Such contemptible scoundrels deserve no pity; they should be hanged publicly, their despicable carcasses left hanging at the cross-roads for at least a month to deter others from committing such a heinous crime."

While Dr. Orhan let off his steam by narrating his pathetic story twenty to thirty times a day, demanding public hanging of unscrupulous doctors who indulged in the unethical practice of buying their colleagues' stolen electro-medical instruments, Dr. Jamil, the celebrated heart specialist of Labour Apartment also kept himself busy telling his own friends and callers how his electro cardiogram had disappeared from his clinic. The words used by Dr. Jamil and the arrangement of his sentences differed slightly from those of Dr. Orhan but the substance of his complaint was exactly the same, and he concluded with identical recommendations:

"Such rascals must be hanged without a second thought. A scapegrace like that has no right to be called a doctor. The swine who does not hesitate to exploit men belonging to his own profession, one who allows a few thousand liras to strangulate his character, has no right to live. Hang such accursed fellows. Sir!"

Let's now listen to a telephone dialogue between two very intimate friends. Dr. Orhan and Dr. Jamil.

"Hullo Jamil! I've been ringing you up for quite some time but your phone was continuously busy."

"I was also trying to ring you up. That's why you found my phone busy. Orhan dear, do you know I've been a victim of gross injustice?"

"And don't you know what calamity has befallen at this end? Last night my electro cardiogram..."

"Mine too."

"O yes?"

"Yes! But imagine what use is this instrument to a burglar. I'm sure he is going to sell it to some doctor."

"I agree. That's why I don't blame the thief in this case."

"I swear I am prepared to buy my own instrument from the thief even if he puts twenty thousand liras as its price."

"But the unfortunate thing is that the burglar is never going to sell you your own instrument."

"Obviously some other doctor will readily buy it from him."

"Such doctors are real rascals. They must be hanged."

"You are very right. If I had my say, I shall unhesitatingly sentence that unscrupulous fellow to be hanged. That will teach a lesson to others."

"Those who sell their very conscience deserve no pity."

"I swear if that cheat of a doctor falls into my hands, I shall tear him from limb to limb."

"OK, Orhan Sahib. Take care!"

"You too, Jamil dear. Please pray that we get our electro cardiograms soon."

"That's just not possible. Who knows which scapegallows is going to buy them."

Despite his reputation as a thief, Istefano always dressed himself well like a gentleman, lest he be suspected on that account. However, the rags he and Freckled Tekin are wearing today leave no doubt in anybody's mind about both being thieves. They engaged a taxi, put two stolen electro cardiograms in it, drove straight to Great Effort Building, stopping about fifty metres short of it. Leaving Freckled Tekin and the two instruments in the taxi, Istefano walked up to Dr. Orhan's clinic. At that very moment, Dr. Orhan was narrating his oft-repeated story to a friend:

"My EKG... police... some mean professional colleague... hang such rascals..."

Dr. Orhan had just said "hang these rascals" when Istefano entered the room. His appearance brought an immediate ray of hope on Dr. Orhan's face.

"Can I talk to you in confidence, doctor?" asked Istefano. Dr. Orhan put his hand on Istefano's shoulder and led him to the examination room.

"Doctor," said Istefano, "I have an electro cardiogram with me. I thought you may be interested in it."

"Let's see it," suggested the doctor.

Istefano whistled to Freckled Tekin from the rear balcony and the latter was soon in the clinic with the stuff for sale. Dr. Orhan had a quick look at it and said:

"How much?"

"You know, sir, it's not available in the market these days."

"Leave that story alone and tell me the price."

"You can see it has been used very sparingly, doctor."

"That's alright, but what's the price?"

"How much can you pay, sir?"

"It is yours, so you should say how much you want for it."

"You can't get it for anything less than fifteen thousand in the market. I shall be satisfied with five thousand."

"Five thousand? That's a bit too much. I know you are selling me stolen goods."

After some haggling, Dr. Orhan purchased Dr. Jamil's electro cardiogram for two thousand liras.

Before long, Istefano was in Dr. Jamil's clinic. Dr. Jamil was also narrating his usual tale to a friend:

"The only way to rid the society of such knaves is to hang them publicly."

The process of bargaining between Istefano and Dr. Jamil took a relatively longer time. In vain did Dr. Jamil try to intimidate Istefano:

"Don't think you are clever enough to befool me, mister! Do you think I have any doubt that this instrument is stolen property?"

The threat did not work. At last Jamil purchased the electro cardiogram of his most intimate friend, Dr. Orhan, for fifteen hundred liras.

Dr. Orhan is talking to a police inspector and a constable who have come to inspect the burglar's finger-prints on the window pane in Dr. Orhan's balcony:

"Inspector! My instrument was destined to be lost; so it has been lost. By now we have even thrown away the broken window pane. You are wasting your time and energy in search of finger-prints."

"Doctor, I am sure the thief is going to sell your machine to a doctor."

(The telephone bell interrupts the dialogue. The caller was Dr. Jamil.)

"Orhan! Jamil here. How are you?"

"I'm fine. How about you?"

"Thanks, I am also fine."

"What can I do for you?"

"O nothing. I just wanted to say hullo and enquire about your welfare."

"Very kind of you, Jamil. I was also thinking of ringing you up at this very moment.

That's what they call telepathy, you know. When do we meet?"

"Let it be this very evening. We'll grab something to eat."

"Very well. See you in the evening."

"Bye!"

This afternoon, Istefano, the technical thief and Freckled Tekin, his aide, were seen closely observing another apartment and the area around it. There is a doctor's clinic on the first floor of this building also.

The Mother of Three Angels

"The heaviest load that a man has to carry and which he cannot get rid of, is his own body," mused the old man, struggling hard to drag himself along. Cars whizzed past him one after another. He was deeply engrossed in his own random thoughts.

"The weaker this wretched body grows, the more burdensome it becomes. What a paradox! And look at those cars. What colours, what designs! I must be fifty kilos? 0 no, not more than forty, at best forty-five!"

He was walking along, thinking, putting questions to himself and supplying their answers. A cough interrupted his chain of thoughts every now and then.

"Could I ever imagine I would find myself in such a pitiable plight? I wish I could buy myself a bun. And what if there were a hot cup of tea as well!"

Cars continued flying past him. Presently he saw a brand new deep blue car and realised that it had slowed down as it went by. A maiden as pretty as a couplet drove the car. Her dark curly hair was dishevelled by the breeze. The old man felt that the charming lady, having slowed down, was gazing at him. He smiled. With the smile, the wrinkles on his sunken cheeks multiplied and deepened. He said to himself:

"The eyes of beauty have at last spotted me, but alas, what an inappropriate time in life to be spotted!"

The glittering new car picked up speed. It had gone hardly fifty metres when it stopped. The miserable old wreck was feeling dead tired but he continued dragging himself forward slowly. As he passed by the blue car, the lady peeped out to have a good look at him. Now there was no doubt left in the old man's mind. It was certainly he on whom the kind glances of love were fixed. How lucky! However, for the old man the idea was too pleasant to be taken as a reality. He thought he was day-dreaming under the adverse influence on his mind, of a hungry stomach.

The blue car moved off again. Again it stopped some distance ahead. The woman was still intently staring at him. The old man thought:

"Surely she has mistaken me for someone else. Or maybe she is feeling pity on me." And then he said jokingly to himself, "Mister! She has undoubtedly lost her heart to you."

The blue car moved, went a few hundred metres and again stopped. The pretty lady's eyes were still tracking him. Her stopping, moving off, stopping again and staring looks made the old man feel quite uneasy. He was extremely impatient to know the exact reason for her curious behaviour.

"Does this lightning really want to strike me? Or is there some other reason that I can't guess?" Thus wondering, he crossed over to the opposite footpath. The lady turned her head and started gazing at him through the opposite window. His doubts began turning into certainty.

"After all, I wasn't all that ugly in my youth," he thought. "As a matter of fact, I could even be called handsome."

He left the main road and turned into a side lane. The blue car followed him. This time, the charming lady stopped the car beside him and said:

"Open the door."

He obliged.

"Get in!" she beckoned.

Under mixed feelings of nervousness and joy, the miserable old wreck hesitated at first, but then, emboldened by a sweet smile from the charming lady, he got in. The car sped off. All the way, neither she spoke, nor he.

The car stopped in front of a massive building. The charming lady led him in. A maid servant greeted the lady, looking at the stranger with suspicion. The lady and the old man entered the hall. Without giving him a chance to sit down, she ordered the old man:

"Undress!"

"Er...er...if you permit me ma'am," he mumbled.

"I say take off your clothes," she shouted.

Reluctantly, the old man removed his filthy, tattered shirt.

"Take off the pants too!" she commanded.

The miserable old man was now dead certain of the jackpot. He became completely oblivious of his hunger and his fatigue.

"A woman is, after all, a woman," he said to himself. How can one predict the behaviour of the human heart, and a woman's heart at that? I am positive this pretty creature has taken fancy to something in me of which I am not aware."

He removed his trousers too and was left with only his undergarments.

The lady pressed a button. A maid entered. Even though a maid servant, she was as pretty as, if not prettier than, her mistress.

"This is utter shamelessness," the old man thought. "It is the height of immodesty for a gentleman to be found in underclothing in the presence of two beautiful young ladies."

The pretty mistress commanded her pretty maid: "Tell the nanny to bring in the children."

The maid went out. The miserable old man was shivering in his underclothes. Was it due to cold or excitement, he did not quite know. He was suddenly reminded of a lady who, long time back, had developed illicit relations with a stranger, merely to avenge her husband's infidelity.

"Maybe this woman too is making me a tool for use with some such motive," he thought, but quickly decided that it was worth becoming a tool in the hands of such a beautiful woman, irrespective of her motives. He therefore stood quiet and waited patiently.

The maid servant reappeared after a while. She was accompanied by the nanny and three children. The eldest was about ten, the youngest about six, two of them girls and the third a boy, all as pretty and innocent as angels.

"One wouldn't bother so much about the presence of the maid and nanny," thought the miserable old man, "but isn't it highly immoral to parade these innocent angels before a semi-naked man?"

His legs were thin as bamboo sticks, his neck as a straw. One could easily count his ribs, even from afar. He appeared like a skeleton stuffed inside a filthy skin and planted there in the hall.

The pretty lady asked the nanny:

"Did Aysel take her meals today?"

"Very little, ma'am," answered the nanny.

"And Goksel?" asked the mistress.

"She has completely lost her appetite, ma'am," the nanny replied. "Even today she has taken nothing."

"How about Altan?" she enquired.

"He just took a bit of chocolate, that's all."

The pretty lady fixed her intimidating glances at the little angels. Then, pointing towards the shivering, half-stripped old miserable, she thundered:

"Look! Do you see that man? Do you see his protruding bones? Remember, if you don't eat all of your full meals, you will be turned into such miserable creatures."

The three angels looked terribly scared. They all clutched at the fleshy thighs of their mother. The mother of three pretty angels turned to the old miserable and ordered:

"Get dressed quickly. You may go now!"

I Committed Suicide

Some time ago, I had suicidal tendencies. I felt disgusted with life. All I thought was to commit suicide.

And this is how my first adventure in that direction proceeded: I asked myself: "O ye romantic patient! What type of death would you like? Will a pistol suit your temperament or a knife? The depth of the sea or the wheels of a train? Poison or?..

An inner voice answered my question: "Mister! After all one dies only once in a lifetime. So why not follow some tried out royal method for a date with death?"

Accordingly, I decided to end my life by taking poison, in the same way as some renowned historical personages had done, lying in comfortable, cosy beds in their royal palaces. It mattered little if I did not possess a cosy bed or a royal palace; my humble house and its brick-lined floor was good enough for the purpose.

Having made up my mind, I headed straight for the chemist's shop, purchased a dose of the deadliest of poisons and returned home. Having locked myself in a room, I sat down to write a long, romantic letter, ending with a sentence which read something like this: "Adieu, thou mortal world!"

And then I gulped a peg of poison down my throat and lied down on the floor. I was expecting all my blood vessels to swell within moments, cutting off the circulation of blood in my body, causing paralytical shivering in my limbs, but nothing of the sort happened. After a long wait, I got up, had another peg full of poison and lied down again. Time passed by pretty fast but I did not feel the slightest sign of poison in my body. It was only later on that I discovered that in our very dear country, where milk is sold mixed with water, butter with mashed potatoes, chillies with powdered bricks, they do not hesitate selling even poison without making it impure! It means a gentleman has no hope in hell to successfully commit suicide by swallowing poison.

Your humble servant has proved fairly mulish by nature. Once an idea takes roots in my mind, sooner or later, I do succeed in putting it into practice. I now decided to blow off the contents of my skull with a single bullet of a pistol, thereby ensuring a guaranteed suicide. I loaded the pistol, placed its muzzle against my forehead, closed my eyes and, with clenched teeth, pressed the trigger. Hello! What's wrong? The bullet didn't go off. I pressed the trigger once more but the result was no different. Experts told me later that my pistol had been imported under the United States military aid programme.

After my disappointing encounter with the pistol, I suddenly thought of gas. That could prove a sure killer. And death through gas is considered fairly glorious. Accordingly, I closed all doors and windows, making sure to plug all holes and crevices with rags, and fully turned on the gas cock. I dumped myself into a chair and tried different poses. At last I adopted a highly dignified pose so that people find me a serious person, at least after my death. The morning turned into noon, afternoon and then evening. There was no trace of the angel of death!

A friend dropped in towards the evening.

I shouted: "Don't come in! Go out at once."

"But what's the matter, mister?" he asked.

"I'm going to die," I said.

"You are not about to die, but I'm sure you are about to go mad alright."

On hearing my plan, he burst into laughter and said:

"You are a fool of the first order, I must say. Don't you know the gas pipes emit pure air now-a-days? If you are really serious about suicide, take my advice and act upon it. Maybe this is how I can pay you back for your friendship."

He advised me to buy a good quality knife, poke it into my stomach like the brave Japanese, and holding my bloodstained intestines in my hands, walk off from this mortal world of flesh and blood.

I thanked him for his valued counsel, went straight to the market and bought a knife. As I held the knife in my hand, I shuddered. If you ask me the truth, the idea of taking out one's intestines with a knife, especially when the intestines happen to be your own, is not very pleasant. Another thought that continued disturbing me was the disgrace and shame that was sure to follow me after my post-mortem examination, when the doctors would fail to find in my stomach or my intestines, the thing they call food, or any semblance thereof. Nevertheless, I held the knife in my armpit and started walking towards my house when two policemen stopped me.

Very seriously, I tried to explain my position to the two:

"Sir, please listen to me patiently. I pay all my taxes to the government with meticulous regularity. I have never uttered a single word against our beloved government. You will rarely come across a more respectable citizen than..."

They interrupted my long talk, snatched the big knife that was peeping out of my armpit and shouted:

"O you respectable citizen! What's this toy doing in your armpit?"

I now realised that I had been unlucky enough to come across that special police squad which starts searching respectable citizens now and then, in order to reduce the ever-increasing incidents of theft, robberies, and other crimes in the town.

I said to myself:

"O God, it was never an easy matter to live in this land of yours, but now it appears equally difficult to die here. How long are we destined to tolerate this high-handedness?"

One should learn from me how to be resolute. Once I have decided to end my life, who on earth can prevent me from doing so? The police confiscated my knife, so what? The very next day, I bought a thick rope from the grocer's shop and rubbed it thoroughly with soap. I tied one of its ends to an iron hook hanging from the ceiling, made a loop at the other end of the rope and standing on a chair, passed my drooping neck through the loop. I then kicked away the chair from under my feet. As soon as the chair fell off, I dropped on the floor with a thud. The rope had proved too weak for my weight. I went and complained to the grocer.

His innocent reply: "Sir, we no longer get the genuine stuff from abroad, how can we then supply genuine stuff to our customers?"

I was thoroughly convinced that it was impossible for me to die. If the search for death has proved so futile, I thought why not make arrangements to live? As a filled stomach is a prerequisite for living, I headed for the nearest restaurant. There I got some omelette and ate them with canned food. And I topped it all with spaghetti. I was fully satiated. As I came out of the restaurant, I was attracted by a bakery on the other side of the road. I went in and swallowed five pastries and cream rolls, one after the other.

A newspaper hawker was passing through the street, shouting:

"Sixteen pages! Full sixteen pages! If you don't want to read, use it to make paper bags. Sell the paper bags and earn a profit. Here comes today's Daily..."

I normally avoid pro-government newspapers. As I had not seen a paper for so many days, I could not resist buying one from the hawker. On reaching home, I was scanning through the paper when sleep over-powered me. While sleeping, I felt as if someone had poked a knife into my stomach. It was a terrible, gripping pain that defies all description. When the pain became unbearable, I started shouting. Someone arranged an ambulance and sent me to hospital. By the time I reached the hospital, I had fainted because of severe pain. When I came to myself, I saw a doctor standing by my bedside.

He said: "You must have eaten some bad food. It was a case of food poisoning. Can you tell me all you had since this morning?"

"I had a few pastries and cream rolls, and..."

"What ..?" He exclaimed. "Pastries and cream rolls, did you say? Have you gone mad? It appears you haven't been reading the newspaper for the last few days. Had you been reading it, you would have never gone near a bakery. And here you are, eating pastries and cream rolls! OK, let's see what else you had today."

"I had my meal in a restaurant."

"A meal? In a restaurant? What did you eat there?"

"Omelette, canned food and spaghetti..."

"Surprising, you are alive in spite of all these! What else?"

"Nothing else, doctor. However, I did read the editorial of a pro-government newspaper. That's when the pain..."

"You got away unharmed. Thank your stars, you are still alive."

While returning from hospital, my mind continued asking me the question:

"If poor people like me are not destined to live a comfortable life, why are we denied a comfortable death?"

Precious Public Funds[*]

A decade is long enough to build a whole town. You are therefore perfectly justified in asking why this hotel building has taken a full decade to complete. Let me explain the reasons.

When the Tourist Department invited tenders, many local and international construction companies gave their bids. The contract was awarded to a foreign firm for reasons best known to the Department itself. Maybe their quotation was the lowest, or they had guaranteed better quality of work. That is an inside story which I don't know. What I know and can tell you with authority is what my mortal eyes have seen happening to this unfortunate structure all these years.

One fine morning, a long time ago, I found my neighbourhood bustling with activity: scores of chairs, red carpets, colourful buntings, a rostrum and long speeches by some high-ranking government officials. The ceremony was followed by a sumptuous lunch for hundreds of guests. The event was given wide illustrated coverage by the press next morning.

Within a few months, foundations were laid, walls went up, and the superstructure was completed. Then one day, a motorcade of staff cars arrived and off-loaded

---

[*] Aziz Nesin has never been to Pakistan. When I first met him in Istanbul, he was keen to know a lot about our constitution and the system of education. I gave him a brief account of our adventures in both these fields. He suggested that I read his story, "Milletin Parasina Yazik." This is a translation of that story. (Translator's Note)

a well-known leading personality (VIP) and his retinue of officials in front of this hotel in the making. While inspecting the building, the VIP stopped in a corridor and enquired:

"Why are the corridors so narrow?"

One of the contractor's engineers replied:

"Sir, all corridors are fifteen feet wide. This width is proportionate to the overall size of the whole structure."

This answer infuriated the worthy VIP who shouted:

"Do you think I have never been to a hotel? During my score of foreign tours, I have stayed in dozens of hotels but I never came across one with corridors as narrow as these. Not only that, the number of corridors is also hopelessly inadequate. The result is obvious: this building does not give the look and feel of a hotel at all. My dear sir, if we are really serious to build a hotel, let us do it properly. Why are we wasting our precious public funds on what can at best be described as an apology for a hotel?"

While the firm's engineer was still fumbling for an answer, the VIP asked his followers:

"Don't you think the number of corridors and their width is inadequate for a hotel?"

"Yes sir," replied one gentleman, "it is inadequate."

"Absolutely inadequate, sir," added another.

"One could say, even less than inadequate," commented still another.

As per the terms of agreement, the contractors terminated the contract and sued the Department for damages.

After months of inactivity, our neighbourhood came to life once again. Demolitions preceded fresh construction. Walls went up again and roofs were laid. The superstructure did not take long to complete. And then came another motorcade. A different VIP emerged from the leading car. The retinue of officials consisted mostly of the same old faces. While going around the building, the group stopped in front of a portal. The VIP went in and asked in surprise:

"What is this place supposed to be?"

"This is a hall, sir."

"What sort of a hall is that?" asked the VIP.

"Sir, it is still incomplete. You will appreciate its beauty after the flooring, plastering and wood-work has been completed."

"I know, my dear, that this is a hall and it is still incomplete. What I want to know is, what the hell are we going to do with such a big hall. Surely you don't want it for horse-racing or for foot-ball matches. This is nothing but a sheer waste of precious public funds."

"But sir," defended the engineer, "this is the size given in the approved plan."

"The plan is not a gospel that cannot be altered. Go and change the plan and that's all there is to it," ordered the VIP.

The fate of their predecessors had made the new contractors wary and wiser. They accepted the modified design with grace and no unpleasantness was caused this time. The hall was reduced in size. The space so saved was utilised to further widen the corridors.

After suspension of work for a long time, construction activity was resumed again. Some demolitions, some alterations, and the super-structure started assuming a new shape. One morning the motorcade arrived again.

As before, the VIP was a different man but his followers were the same old officials. The VIP was full of praise for everything he saw. At the end of his round, he stopped, thought for a few moments, and then exclaimed:

"Where are the domes and the arches?"

"What domes and which arches?" questioned the perplexed engineers.

"Well, isn't it supposed to be a Turkish hotel? Have you ever seen a Turkish hotel with no domes and no arches? Granted the hotel is primarily meant for foreign tourists, but its design must conform to the basic architectural traditions of Turkey."

"But sir, the design has been..."

"Design, design, design!" interrupted the VIP. "This is what happens when contracts of such vital national importance are blindly awarded to foreigners. How do you expect foreign firms to respect and cater for the spiritual and aesthetic needs of the locals?"

At this moment, the VIP posed a question to his followers:

"What do you think, gentlemen?"

"You are very right, sir. Our national requirements, aesthetic taste and spiritual needs must take precedence over all other considerations."

"Domes and arches are a must, sir." added another gentleman.

"What a pity!" lamented the VIP. "This poor nation's meager public funds go down the drain by the millions and nobody is hauled up for gross negligence."

As the demolition and reconstruction of all roofs and doors meant colossal extra cost, prolonged negotiations resulted in a compromise. It was decided to partially sacrifice the spiritual and aesthetic needs of the nation and be content with only a few domes and a few arches. This necessitated a revised design and a modified contract which took another few months to finalise.

At last the work on the site was resumed. Luckily, no visitors came to the site for months. The building was about to be completed when the motorcade showed up again. This ultra-capricious VIP seemed completely dissatisfied with whatever he saw. With a profound expression of grief, he proclaimed:

"What a grotesque design for a hotel! Who on earth ever thought of having so many corridors in a hotel? There are more corridors and less room to live. I bet poor bewildered tourists are going to lose their way and never get out of this labyrinth for the rest of their lives. Whosoever is responsible for this criminal waste of precious public funds, must be hanged in public."

Persistent modifications to satisfy the caprice of numerous VIP's from time to time put back the completion of this kaleidoscopic edifice by many years. The restive opposition press brought forth allegations of wasteage of huge public funds by the government. All this gave an unprecedented boost to the pace of work on the site. But then an unexpected hitch arose and once more the work came to a halt. The problem: should the ceiling be adorned with Turkish marble tiles or decorative bricks, imported from Marseilles for the purpose? After prolonged consultations it was decided that neither bricks nor tiles but terracotta to be used for the ceiling.

Just when the building was being given the finishing touches, the inevitable VIP (a different one of course!) arrived at the scene. He suggested blue Turkish porcelain tiles for some rooms, to add colour to the scheme of things. Before others could comment on his proposal, the VIP was taken aback by the discovery that the hall had no pillars. Looking aghast, he asked:

"Why are there no pillars? How can such a big roof stand without supporting pillars? You don't have to be a prophet to forecast its collapse any moment."

One of the tactless engineers staked his career by volunteering a reply:

"Rest assured, sir," he said. "The roof will not collapse. Everything has been done after detailed calculations of load, stress and strain."

"How can you say that?" asked the VIP, and continued:

"After all, the roofs that do fall, do not fall by miracle, do they?"

And then he questioned the accompanying crowd:

"Don't you agree gentlemen, that this pillar-less roof is going to fall?"

"Yes sir," replied the customary yes-men in unison. "It is certainly going to fall."

Another fellow from the crowd commented:

"It is bound to collapse, sir. Imagine the weight of the huge roof itself, and then add to it the weight of furniture, tourists and their baggage. Only God and pillars can save this roof from falling. It will come down with a thud the moment there is a crowd of people on the top floor."

Like his predecessors, this VIP also shed tears to sympathise with the nation for the loss of precious public funds and uttered unpleasant remarks about incompetent hands that dominated the previous regime.

The raising of pillars took many more months. The leader of a subsequent inspection team objected to the pillars being square-shaped instead of being round. He maintained that round pillars looked more exquisite. To drive his point home, the VIP produced a moth-eaten school textbook containing the picture of a Greek temple with round pillars. Before ordering all square pillars to be rounded, this patriotic VIP also expressed a sense of profound loss at the waste of precious public funds and cursed his predecessor in no uncertain terms.

The next VIP who visited that building before its completion, objected to the narrow and steep staircases. He expressed anxiety over the difficulty that aged tourists were likely to face while using those stairs. He was politely reminded that lifts had been installed for customers' use.

"Then why have the stairs?" asked the angry VIP "Isn't it an absolute waste of public funds?"

I can see you are now becoming impatient. I will not hold you long. Just listen to what happened at the opening ceremony of this hotel the other day. One of the guests at the ceremony happened to be a very famous architect from a foreign country. I had an opportunity to talk to him. After showering eloquent praise on those who had designed and built this magnificent hotel, he remarked:

"Rather than using it as a hotel, I wish your government had offered this building to the United Nations for use as their headquarters."

I did not get the joke, so he explained:

"You know, this beautiful building contains within its narrow confines, architectural designs and styles peculiar to more than half the countries of the world. It can, therefore, legitimately lay claim to the United Nations headquarters. The domes and arches, the blue porcelain tiles, the triangular porch and the wrought iron railings and grills present Turkish architecture; the walls and straight roofs are peculiar to the Scandinavian countries; the modification that has sub-divided the original banquet hall into small cubicles has given it the Arabian tinge; the portal and the main hall with its rounded pillars remind one of the Acropolis. As a matter of fact, the Acropolis is not half as Greek as this grand hall of yours. Similarly, one can find numerous features reminiscent of excellent Italian architecture. The lavatories and bathrooms are typically American in style and fitments. And you don't have to be a connoisseur to detect Indian, Chinese, Russian, and even Japanese architectural influence as you visit various parts of the hotel. I can assure you that if I had not seen this eighth wonder of the world with my own eyes, I would have never believed that human ingenuity could compress so many divergent styles and architectural designs into one single building."

What a Difference

One morning, in a park in one of the towns of England, the police found a man who had been tied to an electric pole with ropes. I shall tell you later who that man was. For the present, just suppose such an incident took place in Istanbul. Here is the sort of conversation you will hear at the site of occurrence:

Watchman: "Who are you?"

(After repeating this question a number of times, he gets no response from the man. He starts blowing his whistle and the police arrives in no time.)

Policeman: "What's the matter?"

Watchman: "Sir, there's a man tied to the electric pole over there."

Policeman: "Who has tied him?"

Watchman: "I don't know, sir. May I untie him?"

Policeman: "No, no! Wait. Maybe the Inspector wants to come and carry out the investigation personally: Go and find out if the man is alive or dead."

Watchman: "I just saw him moving his eyeballs, sir."

Policeman (shouting at the victim): "Who are you, mister?"

(There is no response, so the Station House Officer [S.H.O.] is informed.)

S.H.O. : "Bring him to the police station at once. Also find out who he is. He might be a spy. Keep a close watch on him. Don't let him run away."

Let's now go to England and see what is happening to the man there. Two bobbies untie him immediately and ask him politely:

"May we know your name, sir."

"I'm Arnold Maching."

Both policemen bow with reverence. The name appears to be familiar. One of them asks:

"Sir, are you Mr. Arnold Maching, the famous sculptor?"

"Yes, that's right."

Second policeman: "Are you Mr. Arnold Maching, member of the Royal Society of Sculptors?"

Mr. Maching: "That's right."

First policeman: "Sir, would you take the trouble of accompanying us to the police station or would you like us to drop you at your residence?"

Mr. Maching: "I'll accompany you to the police station."

Let's now come back to our own country. The two policemen untie the man from the pole with the help of the watchman.

One of the policemen thunders: "Come on now, you'll have to go to the police station with us."

Led by two policemen and the watchman, the victim reaches the police station. There is no Royal Academy here, nor do we have any renowned sculptors. But let's suppose that the man is Mr. Hikmet, a famous sculptor of our country. As soon as he reaches the police station, he is addressed by the S.H.O. thus:

"What's your name, mister?"

"Why don't you speak out? I'm talking to you, mister! What's your name?"

"I am called Hikmet, sir."
"What do you do?"
"I'm a sculptor."
"A what?"
"A sculptor."
"I mean what job do you do?"
"I make statues."
"Statues? What kind of statues?"
"Statues of human beings and of animals. I can make all sorts of statues."

You must be tired, but I shall request you once again to accompany me to England because it was there that the actual incident took place. As far as the case here is concerned, you know that I am coining it merely for the sake of comparison. The British S.H.O. is interrogating Mr. Maching:

"Sir, who tied you to the pole? Was it some burglar or a highwayman?"

"No."

"Did some enemy of yours have the cheeks to show you that impertinence?"

"No, sir. As a matter of fact, it was my own wife who had tied me to that pole."

"I beg your pardon! Are you serious that it was Mrs. Maching who did that?"

"O yes."

"Surprising. After all, why should that honourable lady..."

"There's nothing surprising about it. I had myself requested my wife to tie me to that pole and go home thereafter."

"But why, Mr. Maching?"

Before you hear Mr. Maching's reply, come back to Istanbul and see how the S.H.O. here is carrying out the interrogation.

"Then how is it that while you were making statues, somebody tied you to that pole in the park? Did you fall a prey to some brigand?"

"No sir."

"In that case, it must be some burglar who did that in order to deprive you of your cash."

"I'm not a rich man. Nobody would waylay me for the sake of money."

"It's likely that an enemy of yours might have done that to settle some old scores."

"Sir, I'm a citizen of very humble status. I have no enemies."

"Then why don't you tell us who tied you to the pole and why?"

"It was my wife, sir."

"Say again! Was it your own wife? That's really the limit. How cruel can some wives be in this world! Well, if your own wife tied you to the pole, she must have been assisted by her paramour, both being keen to remove you from their way forever."

"Not the least; my wife was all alone."

"What type of a man are you mister? How can a woman tie a man to the pole single handed? Didn't you shout for help?"

"No sir, I kept quiet."

"You henpecked fellow."

"Sir, I had requested my wife to tie me to that pole."

This was good enough to turn a serious interrogation into a boisterous laugh on the part of the policemen. The following story, fed by the police, was published in the local press next morning:

"A cruel wife's misdeeds"

"Last night, a strange incident took place in our town. A terrorist's wife used a clothesline to tie her husband tightly to an electric pole. The husband did not as much as raise an alarm. (For detailed story see page 3). The picture above shows the husband and his sadist wife and it reminds of the happy moments of their life soon after the two were married."

Let's again go over to England where Mr. Maching is explaining to the S.H.O. why he had requested his wife to tie him to a pole.

"As you know, I'm an artist. I'm extremely sensitive by nature. My eyes cannot put up with anything filthy, unartistic or crude. I am particularly averse to crude or unartistic things if they start appearing in the very town where I live. As an artist, it is one of my primary duties to make my town-fellows and countrymen realise the importance of pleasant, beautiful surroundings. Unfortunately, our municipal corporation lacks any aesthetic sense. Consequently, our whole town has been pockmarked with newly-erected electric poles which are crooked in shape and horrible in appearance. These poles neither match with our old buildings and historical monuments, nor do they go well with our roads and streets. Above all, they do not come up to the high aesthetic taste of the town's old inhabitants like me. Compared to these, the old wooden electric poles provided just the right backdrop to the milieu so peculiar to this ancient town. Through the medium of letters addressed to the press, I tried for a long time to convince the corporation why it should desist from their obnoxious plans but nobody cared a fig. As a mark of protest against this extreme vandalism of the corporation, I had requested my wife to tie me to any of those new monstrosities."

At this end the S.H.O. is releasing his steam against Mr. Hikmet:

"There is certainly some screw loose in your upper storey. I have never heard in my life that any person in his senses who had willingly, rather voluntarily, got himself tied to an electric pole, and that too at the hands of his own wife. Tell me, if you haven't gone mad, what else is wrong with you?"

"No sir, I haven't gone mad. With your permission, may I explain my position?"

"Permission be damned! Why don't you go ahead with whatever you want to say?"

"Sir, your humble servant is fed up with this town of yours."

"How funny! Every living person in this world is prepared to lay down his life for this beautiful city and here you are saying that you are fed up with it. That's very odd. If that's really the case, why don't you get out and go elsewhere to carry on with your nefarious activities? But before you leave, tell us what exactly in this town has made you so disgusted with it?"

"The odd buildings, the narrow lanes, the pot-holed roads, the nine-storeyed palaces rising to the skies besides slums, the abundance of horrendous colours, the smoke, the noise .. What else do you want me to count?"

"You appear to be a very strange person. Why don't you go and keep yourself busy with your statues, rather than meddling unnecessarily with all these matters? Do you think you are the mayor of this city?"

"Sir, the disgusting things that I have mentioned are a constant eye-sore for me."

"I got it now! I think instead of being tied to an electric pole, you should have been roped to something else! Suleiman! Hurry up! Prepare this man's documents quickly and take him to the government hospital for a medical check-up."

We are in England for the last time. Newspapers have started a forceful campaign in support of Mr. Maching. His protest has been upheld. All the old electric poles have been removed and new ones have been re-erected in their place.

You must be wondering whatever happened to the gentleman, Mr. Hikmet, who had fallen into the hands of our own police. You might have missed the following insignificant news item that appeared in the press two days after the above incident:

"A lunatic taken into custody"

"An insane person got himself tied by his wife to an electric pole in the town park of our city at midnight on... His contention was that the unaesthetic actions of the municipal council were a constant eye-sore for him. He was arrested by the police and sent for a medical check-up. The doctor's report diagnosed the man as mentally deranged. Accordingly, he has been sent to the lunatic asylum. The lunatic claims to be a sculptor and gives out his name as Hikmet."

Government Secrets Everywhere

My errands for the day included buying some fruit, soap and cheese. While returning from the office, I purchased soap from Spice Bazaar and cheese from the poultry market. I bought a kilo of grapes on the way home. Towards the evening, somebody at home asked me, "Don't you have any writing paper?"

"Why do you ask?" I enquired. "How can I ever be without at least some sheets of paper?"

"Well, if that's the case, why have you been practicing writing on soap bars?" I was asked. And with that question, I was confronted with two soap bars. O yes, both did have something written on them.

But hold on! This was not something written by hand, it was type-written. What the hell? Who on earth ever typed on soap bars? Maybe it is a new advertising gimmick, the brainchild of this particular manufacturer of soap.

I tried to read the message on the soap bars but discovered that it was actually the impression of writing. I taxed my brain a little more and came face to face with an extract from a certain secret official document. The following lines were clearly legible:

"Secret. Personal. Following is a summary of the expert's answers to the questions asked through your cipher message number XXXX, dated XXXX. Because of the classified nature of the contents of this report, it is being sent to you through a special courier."

A strange feeling of uneasiness overtook every member of our family. We had all unwittingly become aware of some highly sensitive official information of a secret nature. While we were still wondering what to do about it, someone came running from the kitchen with a lump of white cheese and exclaimed: "What do you say to this one?"

On examining it closely, we discovered that the lump of cheese too had a type-written superscription. This time, on top of the writing, we could distinctly see two crossed flags bearing a red crescent each. This meant that the writing on the cheese was of a higher security grading than that on the soap.

The already startled members of the family were now completely flabbergasted. The signs of fear on our faces were too obvious to hide from each other. I offered my humble views on the subject:

"This must be a trick. Someone nourishing a grudge against our family must have planned to land us in trouble. Let's immediately get rid of this soap and cheese."

"Let's throw it into the street," suggested someone.

"No, no!" protested somebody else. "If someone sees us, we've had it."

"Then let's give it to the sweeper."

"Have you gone nuts? Give this to the sweeper and you make certain that we are all caught."

A unanimous decision regarding cheese was soon reached. It was agreed that the family members would swallow it immediately, so that along with it the topmost secrets of the government would also be disposed of. Before the swallowing operation commenced, as a precaution one of us stood guard near the window so as to give early warning. You never know when ill luck may catch you, you know. It is always wise to be careful.

How about the soap? Surely we could not afford to swallow these. By about midnight, the whole house started humming with activity. Water was heated and the week's accumulated laundry was all washed in one go. This operation helped us get rid of the soap as well.

We had hardly heaved a sigh of relief when we heard another shout: "Look at this!"

This time it was a paper bag containing grapes that became the centre of everybody's attention. It too bore some official secrets. Everyone in the family was now convinced that we were the object of some malicious trick.

The fear of having landed in trouble sent shivers down our spines. The empty paper bag was at once shown the matchstick. Its ashes were scattered out in the dark lane so as to leave no incriminating evidence against us. We were now fully satisfied that if our house was ever raided, it would be impossible for anybody to find a trace of any official secrets here.

"This is all well and good, but suppose the government insists on having all of us X-rayed?" This was the brain wave of a scared mind.

"But why should the government do that?"

"Suppose they somehow come to know that we are hiding some highly sensitive official secrets in the labyrinths of our intestines. Do you know, every letter of the writing on the cheese we have consumed, which still happens to be inside our bodies, could be distinctly visible on the X-ray?"

But which one amongst us was in his senses to argue that way? We took Epsom salts at once, and every member of the family was administered two spoonfuls each to flush our stomachs and intestines.

I ran to the toilet. Having relieved myself of the heavy load of government secrets, I laid my hand on the toilet roll. And O my God, what did I see there? The toilet paper bore some important clauses of the secret agreement recently signed between an American firm and our government concerning the exploration of oil.

What happened next? Well, I just can't recall that. All I remember is running through the streets at an early hour of the morning in a not very enviable state, with a number of people chasing me, shouting, "Catch the mad man, catch the mad man!"

The Shepherd and the Lamb

Once upon a time, somewhere on the cross-roads of the east and the west, a little closer to the north, a little farther from the south, there lived a shepherd. He had a big herd of sheep and a few sheep dogs. This particular shepherd was completely different from the shepherds that we all know. He was extremely cruel, extremely stone-hearted. He never showed any compassion for others' grief, for others' distress. He never listened to entreaties, nor to supplications. While other shepherds generally carry a flute, this one always carried a club and a whistle. He would draw all the milk from his sheep, shear all their wool, sell their guts, collect their droppings, flay their skins, relish their meat, use their bones, suck their marrow, in short, exploit whatever the poor creatures could offer. And in return for all this, he had nothing but disgust and hatred for his sheep, never showing any sign of compassion for them.

The shepherd used to milk his sheep three times a day, morning, noon, and evening. And yet he always grumbled about their low yield. So greedy was he that nothing could ever satisfy his lust for more. He would go on milking each sheep to the point where, instead of milk, blood oozed out of their teats. Whenever severe pain brought tears in their eyes, or the oozing of blood made them bleat in anguish, the callous shepherd would start showering his thick club on their heads and on their bony backs.

"You mean creatures!" he would shout, "I won't spare you till I have squeezed the last drop of milk out of your shrivelled skins."

Never parting with his club and his whistle, the cruel, greedy shepherd was always anxious to draw from each of his sheep at every sitting, a minimum of forty kilos of milk, even if a poor sheep herself weighed no more than thirty kilos.

The shepherd's cruelties soon became intolerable and the number of sheep in the herd started dwindling day by day. The fortunate ones that died, got away from his torture but the unlucky ones that remained had to pay heavily for the "sins" of their dead comrades, for the avaricious shepherd was bent upon making up every penny of the loss caused by the sheep that had died, from the ones that still lived. He was determined that even if one solitary sheep survived his torture, he would extort from her all the milk and all the wool of the entire flock.

When the shepherd saw that many of the sheep had died, that milk yield had considerably decreased, that the wool and the droppings were no longer forthcoming in previous quantities, he started fretting and frowning, at times behaving like a real mad person. With the club in hand and the dogs in front, he started chasing the sheep across hills and dales.

In the herd there was a small, skinny lamb. The shepherd expected this little lamb also to yield milk, the equivalent of at least twenty cows' milk. But how can a lamb produce milk? While expecting twenty cows' milk from the lamb, the shepherd could not get a single drop from him, and this would make him furious.

One day he was so enraged that he started mercilessly beating the poor lamb. The lamb was so small and so tender that he could not manage to escape from his master's clutches. However, when he could no longer bear the whip, he begged his cruel master thus:

"My dear shepherd! I am a small lamb. My little legs are meant for walking and not for running. I cannot run away from you as the sheep can. I request you earnestly not to chase me and not to beat me."

But the shepherd did not understand the lamb's words.

The shepherd was convinced that the sheep had died because of sheer rancour, that by doing so they had planned to cause him harm, that they had actually betrayed him. He would often thunder:

"Those damned creatures, they have betrayed me, they have let me down, me who used to protect them so well."

And then the shepherd would look at the lamb and wreak his vengeance on him. The innocent lamb was so scared of him and his nasty club that he often remained on the run, trying to keep at a safe distance from the shepherd. He would climb steep, rocky hills to hide himself on bushy slopes. Slowly and gradually, constant running changed the very shape of his hooves, and his legs became abnormally thin and long. This enabled him to run much faster than before. He could now dodge the shepherd with some success. However, the clever shepherd still managed to catch him every now and then. This made the lamb run faster and faster.

The sharp rocks and boulders split his hooves which, with the passage of time, turned into paws having sharp nails. Still the cruel shepherd would catch him at times and give him a sound beating. On all such occasions the lamb would bleat and implore pathetically:

"O my respectable master! I am merely a lamb. Please try to understand this simple fact. I am a lamb and a lamb can never be turned into anything other than a lamb."

But the shepherd did not understand the lamb's words.

Perpetual running for fear of the shepherd's club made the lamb's abdomen sink in. His height increased. Gradually his body started shedding wool which was soon replaced by small, greyish brown hair, just like fur. The shepherd now found it really hard to catch him. The sheepdogs too became virtually helpless. However, the cunning shepherd did occasionally succeed in cornering the lamb and giving him a thrashing, far more severe than ever before. The tiny lamb would again be forced to bleat:

"Worthy master! I am a lamb, nothing but a lamb..."

But the shepherd did not understand the lamb's bleating.

Haunted by the ever-present fear of being caught unawares, the lamb started making better use of his ears so as to sense the danger from afar. He soon learnt how to manoeuvre his ears in all directions. It did not take long for his ears even to change their very form. They now became so sensitive that he could detect the sound of approaching footsteps over long distances.

This would give him sufficient escape time. Even so, he remained vulnerable to the shepherd's mercilessness. The shepherd knew fully well that lambs cannot see properly in the dark. So he started surprising his innocent victim at night. And whenever he did manage to lay his hands on the lamb, he would give him the worst of beatings. As usual, the lamb would have no alternative but to bleat and cry.

"Please, dear master! I'm just a lamb. You are wasting your effort, trying to turn me into something other than a lamb."

But the shepherd did not understand the lamb's language.

The fear of thrashing and the danger of being caught at night forced the lamb to keep awake for nights on end. He would keep his eyes wide open throughout the night, every night. This made his eyes bigger and they soon turned fiery red. Bright as a pair of burning match sticks, his big eyes now enabled him to see everything clearly, even in the darkness of the night.

One serious handicap to the lamb's movement that still remained was his tail. It always got involved in his legs whenever he tried to run fast, to make good his escape. How he wished he never had a tail! This wish of his was granted before long. As a result of fast frequent running, the fat in his tail melted off. He now had a thin, long tail that stood behind him, erect as a whip in the air whenever he tried to run fast, stretching his body to the maximum. The lamb could now run faster than ever before. But whatever he did, he could not always escape from the cruel hands of the shepherd who would now pelt stones at him while giving him a hot chase. On such occasions again the lamb would try to appeal to the shepherd's mercy:

"O my honourable master! I am a lamb. I was born a lamb and I want to die as a ram. What are you trying to force me to become and why?"

At last the lamb started reacting to the brutal treatment of his master. Whenever he found himself cornered in a dark, lonely place, he would not hesitate attacking the shepherd with his newly-acquired paws. The sight of his bruised hands would further infuriate the shepherd. Sometimes the lamb tried to use even his teeth against his master. However, the lamb's wide chin did not permit him to make the full use of his teeth. Nevertheless, he kept trying and, before long, his wide chin started tapering off. Side by side with this, his teeth also started becoming bigger and bigger and his tongue longer and longer.

Although he still bleated, his voice no longer resembled the voice of a lamb. Constant bleating, entreaties and supplications turned it hoarse and thick.

Now the shepherd started inciting his dogs to attack the lamb but even the dogs could not cope with him as easily as of old. With a single, mighty blow of his paws, the lamb would make one of the dogs kiss the ground, pushing the other aside with a sharp bite on his neck.

All this would turn the shepherd mad. His whipping became more callous, more merciless, whenever he somehow got hold of the lamb. In a voice that now resembled growling, the lamb would throw warnings to his master:

"Stop it, O shepherd, or you will rue the day."

But the shepherd did not understand the lamb's threats.

It was a wintry morning. A thick blanket of snow had covered everything in the area. The shepherd woke up early, as usual. He was about to set out for the sheepfold, planning to draw ten cows' milk from each of the few sheep that had managed to survive the rest of the flock. With the thick club in his hand, he stepped out and lo! What does he see? The white snow was spattered all around with red spots, the spots of blood. He looked around and spotted the carcasses of his sheep. All of them had been mauled and torn to pieces. Out of what used to be an enormous flock at one time, not a single sheep was to be seen alive.

Raising one of his hands to his forehead and making a peak for better observation, the shepherd looked afar and there in the distance, he saw the lamb. With all his massive body, it was lying full length on the snow, his forelegs stretched in front. He was trying to cleanse his blood-spattered chin, licking it with his long tongue... The two sheep-dogs were lying dead, one on each side of him.

Presently, the lamb got up. It started moving towards the shepherd slowly, snarling as it approached its erstwhile master. Trembling with fear, the shepherd stepped back nervously, and stammered:

"O lamb, my dear lamb, my pretty lamb!"

The lamb growled back: "I'm not a lamb any more!" The shepherd stammered again: "Lamb, my dear lamb, my pretty lamb..."

The lamb growled back again:

"I used to be a lamb in good old days, but thanks to you, I've become a wolf today."

"But you are my sweet little lamb, my darling lamb, my docile lamb..."

"Alas, my dear shepherd, it's too late now."

And with these words, he pounced upon the shepherd who made a desperate bid to run away. But who could save him from the clutches of the lamb turned wolf? A set of sharp teeth pierced through his neck and his warm, crimson blood was soon sucked by the white snow.

Passers by, who could read the meanings of the red writing on the white snow, learnt of this story about the shepherd and the lamb. And now, for centuries, it has been narrated by people, generation after generation.

Freedom of Expression

You must have come across the series of books titled "Teach yourself..." or "How to..."

Recently I had an opportunity to see a similar series in French. The subjects ranged from the art of making paper and glass to the techniques of overthrowing governments in power and uprooting the strongest of democratic institutions. Each book had been written by renowned subject specialists in a fascinating style. For a veteran journalist like me, the series had a clear-cut message:

"Write a Book on How to Write an Editorial." I made up my mind at once but was soon deterred by a realisation of the innumerable difficulties encountered by an author in getting his works published in this country. As I was determined to let posterity benefit from my rich and varied experience, I did not give up altogether. Instead, I changed my plan of writing a book to one of writing a concise, comprehensive article, explaining all the complexities of the subject which the readers should be able to grasp in one brief sitting. The result, dear readers, is the article that follows. It is the sum-total of my experience of a life time in the field of writing newspaper editorials.

Do you know how I myself write an editorial?

"That's very simple," you will tell me. "Think of an appropriate subject, take your pen and paper, write a few lines on the desired subject, cut a word here, add a phrase there, and then mail off the finished product to your newspaper - that's what you must be doing."

No sir! It is not all that easy. If it were so, every Tom, Dick and Harry would become a journalist. In actual fact, it is a highly complex job. However, I shall make it fairly simple to understand, by illustrating how I myself start, process and finalise my daily task of writing the editorial for my newspaper. I swear that whatever follows is based entirely on facts, that no exaggerations have been added to make the reading spicy.

To begin with, I go through newspapers as a first thing every morning. As I read along, a number of news items convert my nervous tension into high tension. (I am sure the same thing happens to every sensitive newspaper reader.) I then tabulate all the news which has had the most devastating effect on my nerves that morning. These news items provide me anything from ten to twenty appropriate subjects for writing an editorial. Add to this number the subjects brought forward from the previous days and I have a list of about forty magnificent themes, each one of which makes my pen long ardently to write. But alas! All my journalistic ambitions are stifled by the silly restriction that I can write only on ONE subject every day. And that is not all. The single subject to be selected out of a list of over forty has got to be the most harmless one at that. I have to confine myself to a theme, the publication of which should not put the future of the worthy owner of our newspaper in jeopardy, nor direct somebody's wrath upon my own feeble self. It is permissible to discuss weather but in doing so, I must not mention anything about strong winds that may take liberties with the beautiful locks of the "beloved" as that would be considered rude. Similarly, no satire is allowed and no criticism is permitted.

Once I manage to cross the hurdle of deciding on my subject, it takes no time to complete the editorial. And this is exactly when the second phase of my trouble starts. As I emerge from my study with the manuscript in my hand, I am accosted by my better half who appears to have been impatiently lying in ambush. She greets me thus:

"Is the editorial ready, Hasan dear? Let me see today's subject."

Although I always try to smuggle out my writings without my wife's knowledge, I normally do not succeed. As she goes through the manuscript, a deepening melancholy becomes increasingly visible on her face. Her tearful eyes indicate she is approaching the last lines of the editorial. She complains with a hoarse voice:

"Hasan dear, if you care two hoots about your own person, for God's sake think of the risks you are creating for your children's future."

"What's the problem?" I enquire.

"Problem? Could anyone in his senses even think of writing such an article these days?"

"What to do then?"

"Look, why don't you cross out this middle portion of the article? And make this paragraph a little briefer, and change these two sentences to read..."

As the aim of my life has never been to become a hero via journalism, I accept the counsel of my beloved wife and sit down to reshape the manuscript with great effort. I do manage to accommodate at least some of her suggestions when our Prince of Wales appears with a dejected face and says:

"Daddy!"

"Yes dear, what's the matter?"

"Daddy, you have written..."

"What have I written?"

"The editorial that you have written today..."

"O yes, what's wrong with it?"

"You know it's couched in very bitter words. The last sentence is particularly unpalatable. I suggest you eliminate that sentence."

"But my dear fellow, that last sentence is the very essence of the whole editorial."

"Doesn't matter daddy. If you remove that essence, it will be good for the health of all of us."

So I have to remove that last sentence. Next comes my sweet daughter. After spending a few quiet moments standing beside me, she pours out all her affection:

"Daddy," she says.

"Yes darling. What do you want?"

"Daddy dear, see these initial sentences? You should... I mean you should..."

"I should do what? Why don't you come out with what you want?"

"You should eliminate these from the manuscript, daddy."

You must be thinking that by deleting those initial sentences, my day's job would be over. You are sadly mistaken, dear reader. I have still to tackle a neighbour of ours, a highly successful advocate with vast and varied experience. Who informs this gentleman about our domestic affairs has always remained a mystery for me. He has an up to the minute knowledge of everything that happens in our house. As soon as I think I am through with the revised version of my editorial, this gentleman drops in, always trying to indicate that his visit is purely accidental, that he is not there because someone from amongst the members of my own household wanted him to be there. Feigning complete ignorance about the contents of the latest editorial, he says:

"Yes, Mr. Hasan! Let me see what is the theme of your editorial for today."

I must tell you that this gentleman of an advocate always carries a copy of the Safety Act in his right pocket and the Press and Publications Ordinance in his left pocket. Willy nilly, I surrender the manuscript to him. Glancing through it, he adjusts his glasses a couple of times, raises his eyebrows, and then coughing an artificial cough, starts rendering his friendly advice:

"Look here, my dear! You see this sentence? Section 3 (V) of the Safety Act is very very clear about the punishment for writing such stuff... Here it is! It starts with one year's rigorous imprisonment."

I delete the sentence but that does not satisfy the gentleman. He next shows me another sentence in the proposed editorial and warns:

"The minimum punishment for writing this is two years. See this section of the Press and Publications Ordinance."

Accordingly, I omit that sentence too.

The worthy advocate now produces some other law book (e.g. Law of Inheritance, Forest Ordinance, etc.) from the inner pocket of his jacket, and under threat of this or that section of this or that law, advises me to delete certain other portions of the editorial. Being a law-abiding citizen, I go on faithfully following his free legal advice.

Having survived the above mentioned painful incisions, the would-be editorial is up against the toughest of ordeals when God alone knows how the news about the nature of its contents reaches my worthy father. The old man belongs neither to the left nor to the right but he is very fond of reading both leftist and rightist newspapers. He rings me up and directs me to see him forthwith. Interrogation starts as soon as I appear before him.

"What have you written for the paper today? Let me see the manuscript." Every writing of mine draws such comments from the old man:

"Forty long years of life! You have become old alright, but when are you going to become a man, Hasan?"

If matters ever ended with mere scolding, I would be lucky. However, my dear dad sits down with a pen in his hand and inflicts all his ruthlessness on the unfortunate writing of mine. Then, handing back the paper to me, he directs:

"Cross out the portions I have marked."

I am not afraid of the Safety Act or the Press and Publications Ordinance as much as I am scared of my revered dad... I have, therefore, no alternative but to obey his command and delete all that he considers objectionable. With whatever is left in the writing, I proceed to the newspaper office and hand over the manuscript to the owner of the paper.

Did you say the editorial has been written? No sir, not yet. When the owner of the paper reads the manuscript, he raises his eyebrows and enquires:

"Will you never learn how to use a softer language than this?"

"Sir, this article is softer than cream itself. If I make it more soft, it will turn insipid."

"Well, if that is what you desire, I shall delete this part."

The manuscript now lands with the Editor-in-Charge. By virtue of his very appointment, this gentleman must also try his best to effect further improvements in it.

"Mr. Hasan, it will be advisable to make this particular sentence a little less biting," he would suggest.

"As you wish, sir. But if you go through the manuscript with a little more attention, you will notice that the entire vocabulary of soft words that exists in our language has already been exhausted by me."

We both then join our heads to find softer substitutes for words considered too biting by him, and replace the objectionable ones to the extent of our joint success.

"The satirical sting of this last sentence is too sharp. Why not reword it like this..." suggests the Editor-in Charge.

"You may reword it, sir."

"And if we remove this comma from here?"

"You may remove the comma, sir."

After a long session of haggling and compromises, the manuscript is finally cleared by the Editor-in-Charge. I heave a sigh of relief. But I am not one of those lucky fellows whose well-deserved relief lasts long. In less than an hour, my telephone rings.

"Hello, Mr. Hasan?"

"Yes sir."

"In today's editorial, you have mentioned one Mr. Ali."

"Yes sir, I have."

"Mr. Hasan, do you know Mr. Ali is the... of our..? What should we do now?"

"The name does not really matter, sir. You may change 'Mr. Ali' to 'Mr. Vali.'"

"For God's sake, Mr. Hasan. Don't you know Mr. Vali is the... of my better half?"

"In that case, you may delete the name altogether, sir. Just leave the space blank."

My telephone bell rings again after some time:

"Mr. Hasan?"

"Yes sir."

"In the manuscript, you have also talked about... Don't you know we get... from..?"

"If you take... from..., you may delete... also from the draft, sir."

I must be taxing your patience, dear reader, but before I finish, I would like to tell you how my unfortunate editorial looks like after going through all the battering described above. Have you ever seen a bird whose wings have been clipped, whose feathers have been plucked, and whose claws and beak have been chopped off? Well, that is approximately the shape my daily editorial assumes. When it appears in the paper the next morning, you all make fun of it. I too have a hearty laugh at it because I know that the very next day our management is going to issue a contradiction, disowning the contents of even this truncated editorial!

The Ox Tells the Truth

Once upon a time there lived a very rich man called Ahmet. He was a dealer in cattle feed - barley, fodder, etc. Despite being rich, he did not believe in wasting money. He used to run his household most frugally. One day, his wife said to him:

"My dear husband! Our son's shoes have worn out. Can you buy him a new pair?" This made Ahmet furious. He burst out:

"My own mother used to buy me only one pair of shoes in three years. Even then my father used to lose temper on her as according to him, his own father used to buy one pair of shoes in five to seven years. And here is this urchin, wearing out his shoes in only two months. How dare he send you to me for pleading his case for a new pair? One pair in two months!"

"But why are you losing your temper?" asked his wife. "Am I to blame for this? Have I been responsible for wearing out the boy's shoes?" And then, addressing herself to the boy, she continued:

"You useless fellow! Aren't you ashamed of yourself? You should jolly well know that when I and your father were of your age, we never thought of new shoes more than once in two or three years. This new generation has no sympathy towards parents. Hardly two months have gone by and the boy wants another pair of shoes. Tell me, how do you manage to wear them out so quick?"

The boy defended himself:

"But my dear mother, am I to blame for all this? Don't you remember, previously I too used to ask for new shoes once a year? Then a time came when shoes refused to last for more than six months. And now if the shoes become shreds within two months, is it fair to put the blame on my shoulders? Don't you yourself keep complaining that the quality of everything produced in the country has been deteriorating day by day, that the shopkeepers are all cheats, that they sell nothing but rotten stuff?"

Realising the truth in what the boy said, she went straight to the shoe shop and complained about the poor quality of shoes. The shopkeeper delivered a long lecture in his defence, saying:

"Madam, you are just one of my numerous customers who come back daily with the same complaint. As a matter of fact, I am myself ashamed of selling inferior stuff. But are you being fair in putting the blame on my shoulders? You know that times have changed. Pride of performance and sense of achievement have just disappeared. These motives no longer infuse any of our craftsmen. In the whole country you will not find a single shoe-maker who could boast about his craftsmanship."

While she returned home, the shoe merchant went straight to the shoe maker and complained about the deteriorating quality of his work. The shoe maker replied in his defence:

"Sir, are you being fair in putting the blame on my shoulders? Do you know that every day I have to pay more for each item that goes into the making of shoes? I don't mind that, but it's a pity that while prices are going up, quality is going down. In the good old days, producers maintained excellence as a hall mark of their products because they were always keen to jealously guard their reputation. But now, times have changed. Take the case of just one item, leather. The leather that we are getting nowadays is so weak and lifeless that you can turn it into anything but shoes. Surely shoes made of such leather won't last long. Unfortunately, nobody understands this. That's why the entire blame is placed on our shoulders. Be fair, sir, and tell me, what can I do?"

While the shoe merchant returned to his shop, the shoemaker went straight to the leather merchant and, in a bitter tone, addressed him thus:

"Sir, can you give me one good reason why you keep supplying us the most inferior quality of leather? The shoes that we make of it don't last even two months."

"My dear sir, are you being fair in putting the blame on my shoulders?" retorted the leather merchant in his defence. "Do you think I intentionally supply you inferior stuff? I am not such a fool as to annoy old, valued customers like you. Unfortunately, times have now changed. People no longer have any moral scruples, nor are they bothered about their reputation. During the last few months, I have gone from tannery to tannery in search of good leather but believe you me, they are all producing nothing but rotten material. I have no alternative but to sell you the same. After all, I cannot afford to close down my business."

While the shoe-maker returned to his shop, the leather merchant went straight to the tanner who supplied him leather and complained bitterly:

"Sir, the rotten material that you supply brings me unbearable shame at the hands of my customers every day."

The tanner replied in his defence:

"You may be right, dear brother, but are you being fair in putting the entire blame on my shoulders? Unfortunately, times have now changed. Previously, we used to get excellent hides and skins. However, now we can get nothing but the skins of emaciated, starved animals, and at double the previous prices. I just cannot understand what has gone wrong with the moral values of people in this country."

While the leather-merchant returned to his godown, the tanner went straight to the dealer in hides and skins and complained as others before him had done. The hide merchant replied in his defence:

"You are very right sir. I too am conscious of the fact that the quality of hides and skins has deteriorated considerably. However, are you being fair in putting the blame on my shoulders? You should know that our source of supply are the cattle dealers who supply cattle to the butchery. Previously the quality of these hides and skins like the morals of the people of those days, used to be superb. However, times have now changed. Now it is futile to look for excellence, be it in the morals of men or the quality of hides and skins."

While the tanner returned to his tannery, the hide merchant went straight to the cattle dealer and repeated the complaint. The cattle dealer said in his defence:

"Sir, you may be right in your complaint but you are certainly not fair in putting the blame on my shoulders. Please don't forget that I sell the skins of cattle on whom I have absolutely no control. If I sold my own skin and it was found emaciated, you would be perfectly justified in blaming me for its poor quality. The real trouble is that with a steep fall in the moral values of our countrymen, there has been a corresponding fall in the quality of hides and skins as well. It appears that bovine moral values are declining in conformity with declining human moral values. Our cattle seem to be determined to keep in step with their masters. The real fault, therefore, lies with the cattle who supply substandard hides."

While the hide merchant returned to his place of work, the cattle dealer went straight to an ox at a butchery and, holding him by the neck, said:

"Mr. Ox, aren't you ashamed of yourself? Why should you yield most useless quality of hide and put me to shame before my customers? In the good old days, you fellows used to provide excellent, strong hides. What on earth has gone wrong with you chaps now? Why are your hides so lifeless?"

The Ox answered in his defence:

"O brother, you are not being fair in putting the blame on my community's shoulders. The fault is not ours. While we do our best to serve our master, he does nothing to look after us. We know that our flesh, our intestines, our horns, and even our dung are all meant for him, and that in spite of our life-long services to the master, he will not hesitate slaughtering and skinning us one day. We still consider it a sacred duty to offer, as a last present before we die, a good quality skin to the man who feeds us. Unfortunately, times have now changed and, unlike the hides of our forefathers, our skins neither grow in size nor in strength. We feel completely helpless in this regard despite our best intentions because more than half of the barley that we get as feed is nothing but dust and sand. The so-called fodder given to us is nothing but rotten straws and stinking hay full of mud. And to top it all, the quantity of our feed is not even half of what we used to get before. With this state of affairs, I am afraid we cannot offer you any better hides than what you are getting these days. Can you still blame us for this?"

Without replying to the Ox, the cattle dealer returned to his shed. Mr. Ox, feeling aggrieved, went straight to his master and complained thus:

"O master, why don't you look after me? You don't give me enough to eat and whatever you do give me is half adulterated. Consequently, my bones refuse to grow and my hide remains under-nourished and weak. Thus, while the entire responsibility for supplying sub-standard hides to the market is yours, the blame is being laid on the bovine community."

The master replied in his defence:

"You are very right, my dear Mr. Ox, as far as the falling quality of hides is concerned. However, you are not being fair in putting the blame on my shoulders. You know that my small piece of land does not yield enough barley and fodder to feed my whole herd. I am therefore forced to buy the bulk of your feed from Mr. Ahmet, the famous cattle-feed dealer. How should I explain to you, Mr. Ox, that times have now changed and there is not a single person in this country who would care about his reputation or moral values. This rogue who sells cattle-feed has not only doubled and trebled the prices, he has also started indulging in indiscriminate adulteration. This is why you can get neither excellent quality of the past, nor the same quantity."

Although he did satisfy the Ox with the above reply, the master appeared to have been deeply touched by the former's complaint. He went straight to Mr. Ahmet's shop and said:

"Mr. Ahmet, why do you charge exorbitant prices for cattle feed, and for feed that is adulterated at that? I am fed up of listening to the daily complaints of my cattle. The entire fault actually lies with you, but you only blame me."

Mr. Ahmet replied in his defence:

"You may be right sir, but you are not being fair in putting the blame on my shoulders. Please rest assured that I am not responsible for all this. Times have changed you know. People have lost all sense of morality. In good old days, a pair of my son's shoes used to last for a year, but now it wears out in less than two months. And the trouble is that I have now to pay twice or thrice its previous price. The malady is not confined to shoes alone. Take cloth, foodstuffs, household goods or for that matter any item of daily use. There is a two to three hundred percent rise in prices. Quality has deteriorated and adulteration is the order of the day. To be able to earn two square meals for my family under these circumstances, I too am forced to do what others are doing daily to me. I indulge in these practices under the force of circumstances. Please tell me, can I be justifiably blamed for this?"

The next day, Mr. Ahmet went to the shoe-merchant in anger; the shoe merchant in turn went to the shoemaker, the shoe maker to the leather merchant, the leather merchant to the tanner, the tanner to the hide and skin merchant, the hide and skin merchant to the cattle dealer, the cattle dealer to Mr. Ox, Mr. Ox to his master who again went to Mr. Ahmet. Each complained to the next and each got the same reply:

"You may be right but you are not being fair in putting the blame on my shoulders. Times have changed, you know. People have absolutely no moral scruples now. Nobody cares for reputation. You tell me, can I be justifiably blamed for all this?"

Being Late For Work Competition

The new season started in our city the other day, with the late comers' competition. The competition organised amongst the officers and staff of the Directorate General of..., could not be a complete success because only one third of the total strength could participate in it, the rest having reported sick in order to witness an important football match fixed for the same morning. The Director General himself had informed his private secretary a day in advance that he would not be able to attend office the next day because the gear-changing stick of his car was going to be stuck. And since the Director General would not be in office, the private secretary would make use of the opportunity to go and check up the new premises being acquired for the office.

Despite lean attendance, some very interesting results were recorded. There were many claims and counter-claims, but the final official results were as under:

1. As usual, the office doorman arrived first of all at two minutes past eight.

2. Mr. Shaban, the general attendant arrived next. This was at 8.40. He was followed by Miss Aysha, the office maid, and Mr. Rustam, an ex-despatch rider but now a junior clerk. Both came just before nine.

3. Most unusual was the case of Mr. Memduh, who broke his own record of coming early to office. Never in his whole life had he reached his office as early as 9.10. It transpired that the reason for his coming so early was the quarrel that his wife had with him that morning, at

the end of which she chased him right up to the main road leading to the office.

4. Mr. Basri arrived at five past ten. As he is a newly-married young man, the judges condoned his fault. He was followed by Miss Belma Untouched, who has been a typist all her life for she is neither good for the eyes nor for the palate. Miss Ayten Undrowned, a pretty official, was also as late as ever, recording 10.45 as her arrival time. Being prettier than Miss Ayten, Miss Nurten Ball was entitled to come even later than the former. She arrived at ten to eleven.

5. Zeki Sekmez, an unfortunate low-paid employee, whose mother-in-law has died three times, beating her husband who had died only twice, had no alternative this time but to make his father die again, irrespective of the fact that the poor soul has been inhabiting his grave for the last twenty years. He came to office with this sad news at eleven and asked for permission to leave immediately for the old man's last rites. From office, he dashed straight to the stadium to witness the second fixture for that morning!

6. Being a section chief, Mr. Nazmi just peeped into the office at 11.10. This is his usual routine whenever an important football match is scheduled for a working day.

7. There are many people on the staff of offices whose duties are not clearly defined, though their emoluments are specified to the last penny. One such person is Mr. Izzet. You know government servants cannot participate in political activities. In this case, it was the non-political activities of his political party that kept him from attending the office on time. He reached the office at 11.30.

8. The attendance register showed Mr. Melih having reached office at nine o'clock sharp, though everybody knew he actually arrived at quarter to twelve.

9. The late-coming register showed that amongst the female staff, lovely Malahat came at three seconds past 11.50. Nobody has been able to beat her for the last two consecutive years. She has also been three times our national champion in late-coming.

10. Ismail Jan exceeded his drinking limits the night before and although he did manage to grope his way through to his house towards the early hours of the morning, he could not wake up in time to go to office. "Wife's sickness" came to his rescue when he reported for duty the day after the competition.

11. Mr. Matin is an employee who is always on leave. He is seen in the office on the first of every month in front of the pay master's window, receiving his emoluments. And why not? Isn't he the son-in-law of the boss. How about Mr. Mustafa? Did he come at all? Perhaps he did not. In any case, it was not clear what time he came, if he did.

12. Mr. Orhan could not attend office as he had to go to the airport to receive Mr. ... Since lining up for reception of VIP's has been officially prohibited (as it militates against the dictates of democracy), he generally produces a medical certificate the next day to justify his absence.

If the efforts being made in the country to improve standards of late-coming are any criterion, and the highly disciplined training being imparted to all government officials is a true index, it can be strongly hoped that we shall establish a world record in late coming when the next international competition for the same is held.

I am Sorry

"Police! Police!! Help! Help!"

Everybody in the street stopped. People started gathering around him. Although there were policemen amongst them, they ignored the poor man's appeals for help and walked off, bulldozing their way through the crowd.

"Police! Police!" he repeated.

How strange to see a man shouting non-stop for police and despite being there, no policeman going forward to his aid. Even the constable standing on the footpath right in front failed to budge. Surely he must have heard the man shouting in distress, using both his hands as a megaphone to ensure his voice reached the farthest place.

At last the man took courage and, dashing through the mob, approached the policeman on the footpath.

"Please, dear brother, come with me," he implored.

"What's the matter?" enquired the policeman.

"A man is going to be murdered in that building over there."

"I'm sorry, I can't interfere in this matter."

"But why?"

"Because I am a police officer controlling the traffic. If I leave my post, who do you think will look after the traffic muddle?"

The man started shouting again:

"Police! Police! Is there nobody who can save a precious human life?"

Another policeman was seen hurriedly passing by. The man ran after him and said:

"Listen my dear brother! They are going to murder a man over there. Please accompany me. It's not far off."

"I'm sorry, I can't help you. This case lies in the jurisdiction of the Crime Branch, whereas I am working in the Passport Branch these days."

Flabbergasted, the poor man started running around, shouting all the time at the top of his voice:

"Police! Murder! Help!"

Before long, he saw another policeman coming from the opposite direction. He ran towards him:

"My dear brother!" he entreated. "For God's sake, come with me. A murder is going to be committed."

"I'm sorry! I've been detailed by the Home Office for the personal protection of some foreign VIPs."

The crowd was swelling every moment. Someone saw a policeman a few metres away, preparing a ticket against a vegetable vendor. The man in need of help ran towards him as fast as he could and shouted desperately:

"Please come quick! A man is going to be hacked to death in that building across the street."

"I'm sorry! I can't intervene. These days my duty is to check the rates of vegetables fixed by the Municipal Corporation. I also have the additional duty of ensuring sanitation of this area."

What a pity. So many policemen roaming about but none prepared to come to the poor soul's rescue. He started shouting again:

"Police! Help! Murder! Police!"

Luckily another police constable appeared on the scene. To avoid disappointment, this time the poor fellow himself asked the constable:

"Excuse me, Sir. May I know your exact branch?"
"I'm from the Crime Branch."
"Thank God! In that case, dear brother, please hurry up and follow me to that house across the street. They are going to kill a man there."
"I'm sorry, but I can't help you. My job pertains only to theft cases."

The man was utterly disappointed. He started running. On the way, he came across still another policeman. He implored for urgent help to prevent murder in a house not very far off. The policeman regretted:
"I'm sorry, I can't interfere."
"Didn't you say you belonged to the Crime Branch?" asked the man in disgust.
"I did, but I deal with prevention of smuggling, not murders."

The man in distress ran back. By now the street was bursting with spectators. He was fortunate enough to spot another constable.
"Are you from the Crime Branch, Sir?" he enquired.
"Yes."
"Are you concerned with the prevention of murders?"
"I am."
"Thank goodness!" he sighed in relief, and begged:
"Please come quickly with me. They are going to kill a man."
"Where?"
"Over there, in that street, inside the third building."
"I'm sorry, I can't do anything about that. That street falls in the jurisdiction of police station 'B' whereas I am serving in 'C' division."

The last flicker of hope had vanished. Completely stunned, he started back. And lo, there was another policeman!

"Excuse me, dear brother. Do you belong to the Crime Branch?"

"Yes."

"And your responsibilities include the prevention of murder?"

"O yes."

"Is that street across the road within the jurisdiction of your police station?"

"It surely is, but what's the matter?"

"For Heaven's sake, hurry up and come with me. There is going to be a murder..."

"I'm sorry, I can't intervene. I'm on leave today."

He was still wondering what to do when a man approached him and confidently whispered into his ears:

"My dear brother, I too have tasted what you are experiencing today. Who on earth can find a policeman by running about like this? If you really want the police to come right to your feet, go to that open space across the road, stand on a soap box and start delivering a forceful speech. As a matter of fact, you don't have to deliver even a full speech; just utter the sentence: How disgraceful to be living like this!"

The man immediately acted on his well-wisher's advice. With great gusto, he started off from the soap box:

"Fellow countrymen! Isn't it disgraceful living like this in our own country? Had any one of you experienced these things before?"

He wanted to say a few more things when some persons stepped forward and held him by his collar, his arms and his ears.

One of them ordered:

"Come with us to the police station."

"But who are you all?" he asked in amazement.

"I am a police inspector, and these others are my men from the Political Branch."

One of those men started blowing a whistle. The first person to respond to the voice of his whistle was the policeman who was supposed to be on leave that day and had expressed his inability to help. Then came the constable whose jurisdiction extended only within the limits of police station "C" division. And then, one by one, the policeman who was concerned only with the market rates and sanitation, the one attached to the Passport Office, the one caring for the security of foreign VIP guests, and many more. All of them gazed curiously at the man who had requested them for help a few minutes earlier.

Amongst the crowd, he spotted his well-wisher who had advised him to deliver a speech.

"Do you also belong to the police department?" he asked him. "Yes, I am the station house officer."

While escorting him to the police station, the police posse passed by the building where a lot of human blood had already been shed. A seriously wounded, profusely bleeding man was lying on the ground, in dust. On seeing him, the man in police custody heaved a deep sigh:

"Alas! What a pity! Poor innocent soul."

"Was he a relative of yours?" asked the inquisitive traffic constable.

"No," he replied. "I didn't even know him. It was out of sheer human sympathy and fellow-feeling that I was shouting for police to save his life."

The constable entrusted with Municipal functions pushed him forward with a kick and thundered:

"Step out quick! This wretched man's blood is flowing all over the street, spoiling the sanitation of my area. After delivering you to the police station, I'll have to come back to issue him a ticket for this offence."

A Stray Dog Named Tarzan

Our house is in Ankara at Maltepe. Although we don't belong to this city, we have been living here for a long time. Ours was the third house to be built in Maltepe. Originally it belonged to my aunt. We moved and settled here when she died.

Our locality has a dog called Tarzan. We don't know when and from where it first landed here. Perhaps it has been here since it was still a pup. Nobody knows its age either. Ask someone about it and you will be told:

"When we came to live in Maltepe, Tarzan was already here, a full-bloomed dog."

However, that doesn't give even a rough idea of Tarzan's age. We ourselves came to settle here eighteen years back, and found Tarzan a old dog. Our neighbours, the Memduh family, moved to this locality twenty-one years ago and they too found Tarzan here, again a fully grown dog. According to Ilyas, the grocer, Tarzan is past thirty, because when he occupied his present house thirty years ago, he remembers having been greeted by Tarzan who had long passed its puppyhood. Mr. Mehmed, a railroad watchman, says Tarzan is over forty, for when he came to settle down in Maltepe, he says Tarzan was at least three or four years old. Duriye aunty always insists that she is younger than Tarzan. By that account, Tarzan should have been long past his fiftieth birthday.

Nobody knows who christened this dog, Tarzan. It appears that Tarzan itself has been going around to every new-comer in Maltepe, saying: "My name is Tarzan!"

Tarzan has short, brownish hair. It is neither too big, nor too small, just a medium sized stray dog of the familiar type. It isn't lame but is invariably limping. The street urchins always pelt stones on it and often give it a thorough beating. As a result we have never seen even one of its four feet uninjured. Tarzan is the primary plaything of the children of our locality. You see them riding it, without the poor creature ever raising a word of protest. Rather than protesting, it struggles hard to carry the rider despite its bent back. The kids do not suffice with that; sometimes you see two of them trying to ride it together, causing injury to the poor soul's spine. It twists and turns but cannot straighten itself for days and has to drag itself about in the dusty streets.

The younger lot of children derive special pleasure from pulling Tarzan's tail or driving nails here and there in its body, but it keeps standing in front of them as if it wasn't a dog but a mere sheep. When the pain becomes unbearable, it turns its head towards its tormentors, its dirty, yellowish eyes begging for mercy. In worst cases, it may start emitting a painful sound, hardly resembling a yelp.

The kids' most enjoyable game is that of pelting stones on Tarzan. At times, they fix it up against a wall and use it in place of a proper target for improving their skills at "arms."

While returning home one evening I saw fourteen children, with stones in their hands, all lined up and waiting. And then, a rough-looking youngster shouted: "Fire!" The boys fired a volley of stones at Tarzan.

"What are you doing?" I enquired.

"Uncle, we are playing the firing squad," they replied. Well, aren't they children and don't children have the right to play? Didn't we ourselves play with Tarzan when we were of their age?

Do whatever you may to Tarzan, it won't leave this locality. It has become a permanent fixture of Maltepe. Do you think the grown-ups are kind to him? Far from it. Every resident of Maltepe considers it one of his basic civic duties to throw at least one stone a day on Tarzan. If ever it goes anywhere near a grownup person, it is sure to get a kick, strong enough to send it rolling to the ground. I don't recall having ever seen Tarzan without some injury on its body. In our childhood, our friends had cut off its ears. Those who came after us, excelled us by depriving it of its tail.

How does Tarzan fill its tummy? This is a great enigma. It never leaves our locality, nor do the residents of Maltepe ever spare a piece of stale bread for it. It is not known what it eats or what it drinks. As a matter of fact, none of us has ever bothered to think about this.

Once the municipality staff came around to kill stray dogs. Have you seen how they do this? A truck comes and from the truck out jump the dog killers, each holding a gadget about two metres long, resembling tongs or scissors. The two pincer-like prongs of the instrument are very sharp. The dog is chased and caught by the pincers, its two prongs pierce through the victim's abdomen. And then the injured, profusely bleeding dog is thrown into the truck.

The municipal dog-killers captured our Tarzan with the same instrument. We, the people of the entire locality, had all assembled to watch. When the two sharp prongs of the pincers pierced through its abdomen, Tarzan produced a sound as if weeping. It then turned its head and glanced towards us. The dog-killer lifted it in the air with his pincers and while he was about to shove it into the truck, something unexpected happened. Tarzan's abdomen got ripped, enabling it to get disengaged from the grip of the two prongs. With a bleeding abdomen and an unbelievable agility, Tarzan disappeared from the scene.

The next day Tarzan was there again. It dragged itself about with a ripped abdomen but was alright within days.

It was complained to the municipal authorities that killing of dogs in this crude manner was inhuman. Thereupon, the municipal staff started shooting stray dogs with fire arms. One day the dog shooters came to our locality also. It was enjoyable watching this game. All pet dogs had been locked up by their owners. Tarzan did not prove a very difficult target to hit. It got a bullet on its left shoulder and collapsed. Before the dog shooters could pick it up, it managed to escape despite the bullet wound. And it was soon back in our locality, along with its fresh injury.

The dog shooters, by mistake, killed a pet dog. As that unfortunate victim belonged to an influential person, the killing of dogs by fire arms was also declared inhuman and the municipal staff started using poison for the purpose.

One day the dog poisoners came to our locality also. They went around throwing poisoned meat to the stray dogs. Three dogs, including Tarzan, partook of the poisoned meat and fell down within minutes, kicking and shaking. Two of the dogs had their owners who tried to save them by feeding them on yoghurt mixed with garlic. Both died. Only Tarzan survived. We had all thought

Tarzan too had died because nobody had tried to save it. We had watched it twist and turn till the nightfall and were surprised to see it up on its feet the next morning. The children cried: "Long live Tarzan!" and started pelting stones on it.

An American family moved to Maltepe. Their arrival brought good luck to Tarzan. At first, the fourteen year old son of the Americans started feeding it. And then the family built a small kennel in their lawn and gave Tarzan a place to live! Within three or four months, Tarzan was a different Tarzan altogether. It became plump, with bright eyes and shiny hair. When Tarzan became so attractive, we all started liking it. Who wouldn't like a pretty dog? Even the street children started feeding it on bits of bread. And not bread alone! If meat was cooked in a family, the lady of the house would gather the bones and tell her son, "Go, throw these to Tarzan."

By and by there was a growing number of people who would serve Tarzan meat and broth. None of us ever left Tarzan out of our thoughts. One would often hear platitudes like:

"Make sure Tarzan gets water to drink. The poor animal has a tongue alright but it can't ask for water. Let it not die of thirst."

The Americans started bathing Tarzan every two or three days. It became smart, bright and shiny. This made every woman of our locality keen to give Tarzan a bath.

Then came winter and the Americans moved Tarzan to their basement. Before they did that, the people of the locality had long been muttering their displeasure:

"These wretched Americans are going to make sure that the innocent animal is frozen to death."

"Can a dog survive such a severe winter, living out there in the lawn?"

Winter was over. In spring, the American family was to return to the States. We heard they were planning to take Tarzan with them. This caused a great tumult in the locality. The residents had every right to protest. Mr. Mehmed, the railroad watchman, shouted with anger:

"Nobody can take Tarzan from here. After all this is the only dog of the entire locality. That isn't a joke."

With tears rolling down her eyes, Duriye aunty sobbed:

"It was born and brought up in my own hands. I can't part with my sweet Tarzan. No, no, they cannot take it away. We only allowed them to keep it while they were here, and that too because we didn't want them to be deprived of this pleasure; but how on earth can we allow them to take it to America? I'll ruin them if they tried to."

Ilyas, the grocer, also jumped in:

"How can a third party arbitrarily decide whether Tarzan is to go to America? For once, the dog is mine. It was me who brought it up right from the time it was a small pup."

Mr. Memduh, the most enlightened person of our locality, talked in legal terms: "Don't you worry folks. They cannot take Tarzan anywhere."

"Why not?" we asked.

"Because it is against the laws of this country. Tarzan was born here and it has been brought up here. How the hell can they take it to a foreign country when it has no passport?"

Ayten, the typist, expressed her pity for Tarzan:

"Oh my dear Tarzan! What will he do in a foreign land? The poor fellow is not used to the food and water of that country; it's not used to the climate of that country. If it were a human being, it could come back if it didn't like the place, but how can an animal do that?"

An intense anti-American feeling developed in the area on account of Tarzan. The issue was one day going to result in a major tragedy. Ozgur, a university student of Maltepe, was reported to have said, while chatting in a restaurant:

"Let them take away Tarzan... If nothing else, at least the poor fellow will get freedom."

For these remarks of his, Ozgur was about to be lynched by the angry public. Remarked one:

"Hmm... the poor creature will get its freedom? What on earth do you mean by this, you rascal?"

"Wait a minute," Ozgur pleaded. "Please don't misunderstand me. Let me explain what I meant."

He could only manage to say these words when they attacked him, causing injuries to his head and his eyes. Ozgur managed to escape from the crowd with great difficulty.

Assembling in front of the Americans' house, we would all shout in unison: "We want Tarzan, we want Tarzan." However, the Americans would take no notice. At last the headman of the area took the issue in his own hands. He led us to the police station where we complained that the Americans were taking away our Tarzan. The police inspector too was annoyed. He asked us to give a written application and promised to take action on it.

Everybody in the locality wrote an application, each claiming to be the owner of Tarzan. In addition, we started a signature campaign in the area to the effect that we were not prepared to part with our Tarzan. Everybody became a witness to the claim of everybody else that Tarzan belonged to him. Things took a more serious turn when the people of the adjacent locality also started meddling in the issue.

At last the Americans started selling their household stuff. We now knew for sure they were preparing to go. We assembled in front of their house. The American put Tarzan in his car. He thought he would quietly slip off to the airport and fly back home with our Tarzan. But when he saw the crowd, he proposed:

"Take fifty dollars and sell Tarzan to me." These words were enough to infuriate us.

"What does this American think of himself? Just because he has dollars in his pocket, he thinks he can buy whatever we possess?"

"Not fifty dollars, mister. Even if you give a hundred or thousand dollars, we won't give you our Tarzan," we retorted.

At this time, Tarzan gave us very strange looks. It appeared as if he was beseeching us: "For God's sake, save me from the hands of these Americans!" The women and the children started weeping and shouting. The police arrived. They knew the Tarzan issue. One of them said to the Americans:

"Eh, mister! You cannot take away Tarzan."

"Why not?" queried the American.

"Because it has its owners," replied the policeman. Thus, it was only with police help that at last we retrieved our Tarzan from the Americans' clutches.

The Americans departed, their eyes fixed on Tarzan. Tarzan was ours once again. Within ten days it came back to its original form, a mere skeleton, with injuries here and wounds there. It was once again just the dog of our locality. Now from morning till evening, children kept pelting stones on it, piercing nails through its body at various places, riding it in ones and twos.

The other evening, while returning home from work, I saw that the children had tied Tarzan with ropes, upside down on a tree; they had knives in their hands.

"What are you up to boys?" I asked them. It transpired that their teacher had dissected a frog in the classroom to show them its heart. The boys were now going to perform the same experiment on Tarzan.

After this last operation, Tarzan moved about with its wounds and injuries for a few days but then it recovered. You can now see it dragging itself about in our locality, if you happen to pass that way.

The Donkey and the National Service Medal

Once upon a time, a great king ruled a certain country. For a long time, his subjects enjoyed the fruits of prosperity under his benign rule. Everybody lived a contented life. People had no problems and no headaches. The king's government was so democratic that one would imagine the first flower of democracy that ever blossomed in this world, did so in that country.

Time went by, and then something went wrong, God knows where, and this great country found itself in the grip of a vicious famine of unprecedented magnitude. So severe was the famine that even the richest of the king's subjects, whose cellars used to be flooded with the choicest of foodstuffs, started begging for crumbs of bread to satisfy their hunger. The king was quick enough to realise the gravity of the situation. He rightly apprehended that the back-breaking famine would soon incite his subjects, even the most loyal amongst them, to revolt. At last his fertile brain hit upon a unique solution. He sent drum-beaters to all corners of his kingdom, to announce a royal decree:

"Listen to this important announcement carefully, my dearest subjects, and let it not be said that you did not know about it. His Majesty has long been aware of the innumerable meritorious services rendered to this nation by a vast majority of our worthy subjects. As a token of recognition, we have now decided to institute a National Service Medal of different categories. Anyone of our noble subjects who has ever served the national cause in whatever sphere of life and whoever has a claim to the proposed medal is hereby directed to report to the Royal Palace where he shall be decorated at a Royal investiture ceremony. The investiture shall be held daily and shall continue till all our deserving subjects have been decorated!"

This decree worked miracles. Starving multitudes forgot all about the high prices of commodities, the ever increasing shortage of foodstuffs, and the emaciated faces of their hungry kith and kin. Every citizen became preoccupied with a single obsession - how to get a national service medal of the highest order. The king commissioned his work-men to prepare a variety of big and small medals. The size and preciousness of the material of a medal was to be commensurate with the nature and excellence of services rendered by the would-be recipients. Thus, for instance, medals of the first order, meant for the highest category of service, were made of pure gold, those of the second order of pure silver, followed by medals of rolled gold, bronze, copper, brass, iron, tin, etc. etc. The claim of each citizen was duly vetted and his entitlement to an appropriate category of medal decided personally by the king, assisted by his council of advisors and selected courtiers. There was no bar to a citizen getting more than one medal, if his services so justified.

Within a few months, so many citizens had been awarded so many medals that the country's entire stock of metals was depleted. To meet the never-ending demand, non-metallic materials like leather, wood, etc., had to be used. Very soon, the entire population could be seen parading the streets and bazars of all towns and villages, proudly displaying their protruding chests, heavily decorated with all types of medals jingling like the tinklers around the neck of a washerman's ass. Complaints of hunger were to be heard no more.

One day, a cow in the country's capital noticed that the chests of men no longer wore the vacant look of the past, that the prominent ribs of emaciated human beings were now covered up by strange looking bits of attractive materials. Her inquisitiveness drove her to probe the matter further. She liked the idea of royal recognition of service rendered by men. However, she wondered why animals should be denied the same. Although the poor thing had been suffering the pangs of hunger for days and her sagging flesh had left her ribs exposed, the news about medals raised the cow's morale sky high. She took courage and repaired straight to the royal palace. When the guards stopped her at the gate, she mooed:

"Let His Majesty be informed that from amongst his loyal subjects, a humble cow requests for royal audience."

The guards tried their best to turn her away but in vain. At last the king was informed. He ordered the cow to be led in.

"What brings you to the royal court, O Cow?" asked the King.

"Your Majesty," replied the cow, "I have heard that national service medals are being awarded to every citizen of this great country. I am also a claimant for the same."

Considering the cow's demand a sacrilege, the king shouted angrily:

"You stupid cow, how dare you damage the sanctity of the royal awards by such a silly demand? I could never imagine an insignificant quadruped like you could have the audacity to lay a claim on the national service medal. What services can you boast of, anyway?"

The cow mooed humbly:

"Your Majesty, if a cow cannot be a rightful claimant to this medal, nobody else in this country can be. I served Your Majesty and all Your Majesty's worthy subjects all my life. My milk, my flesh, my hide, and my bones are all dedicated to human service. Even my dung is put to innumerable uses by man. What else is needed to win a medal, O Master?"

The king was pleased with the cow's answer. He forthwith conferred a National Service Medal Class 2 on her.

On her way back from the royal palace, the happy cow was accosted by a starving mule:

"Good day, sister cow."

"Good day," she replied.

"You seem to be in pretty high spirits this morning. And what on earth is that glittering tag doing around your neck?"

The cow proudly explained the whole episode. Without wasting another moment, the mule galloped off to the royal palace and demanded immediate audience with the monarch.

"That's impossible," insisted the guards. However, the mule stuck to his traditional mulishness and refused to leave without seeing the king. To add strength to his demand, he gave a couple of nasty kicks to the guards, and a few more to the walls and gates of the royal palace. The king was immediately informed of the arrival of this insolent guest.

"Let him in," ordered the king. "After all, a mule is as good a subject of ours as anybody else."

The mule was shown the way in. Bending on its knees, it wished the ruler a long life and then prayed for the award of a medal. The king enquired:

"O mule, what services have you rendered to this nation that may warrant the grant of a medal to you?"

"Your Majesty," replied the mule, "Isn't it a pity that with all your worldly wisdom, you are not aware of the services rendered by this humble servant of yours. I'm sure you know who carries the heavy guns and ammunition of your soldiers on steep and narrow hilly tracks, keeps your troops supplied with rations and clothing, and conveys a majority of Your Majesty's subjects from one place in the country to another, both in peace and war. Had it not been for the hard working community of mules, the independent democratic existence and prosperity of this great country would have been jeopardised."

The king appeared convinced of the genuineness of the mule's claim. He sanctioned a National Service Medal Class I.

The mule was ambling back happily from the Royal Palace when he was greeted by a donkey:

"Good day, my dear nephew," said the donkey.

"Good day, uncle Ass."

"Where are you coming from, in such a fine mood?"

The mule narrated the story to the donkey. Without wasting a single moment the donkey darted off, stopping nowhere short of the royal palace. The guards tried to scare him off and the sentries tried to dissuade him from his mission but the donkey insisted on seeing the king. At last the king was informed. He ordered the donkey to be brought in. By now, the king had become fed up with the requests of men and animals for medals. As soon as he saw the donkey he shouted:

"You silly ass, have you forgotten the hard fact that you are a mere donkey and that a donkey has no business to insist on having an audience with the king? The cows serve the nation with their milk, flesh, hides and bones; the mules carry loads and passengers in peace and war; but what do the donkeys do, except for braying day in and day out?"

The donkey was fairly disappointed at this unexpected treatment at the hands of the sovereign but he did not give up. He said with due respect:

"Your Majesty, It's only the asses that serve you best. If this country did not have thousands and thousands of asses like me, how on earth could you continue ruling this nation as a monarch in this age of democracy? Your Majesty should be grateful to asses, with whose active support you have remained the undisputed ruler of this country for such a long time."

The king thought over the donkey's assertion for a while. Then he looked around, intently watching every one of his advisors and all his courtiers. He seemed convinced that the donkey was right after all. His anger turned into a sweet smile and he said:

"O donkey, the loyalest of my subjects, I do give credence to whatever you have said. Unfortunately, I have no medal worthy enough of your meritorious services. However, I hereby decree that as long as you live, you shall be a state guest, with a permanent right to one sackful of hay from the royal commissary every day. So eat, drink and be happy but do keep yourself busy in braying and praying for my long life and for the security of My Majesty's benign rule."

Agent 0X-13

During his long career in many important countries of the East, he had been responsible for the planning and execution of scores of highly complex and sensitive intelligence missions for his country- His brilliant success in spying and sabotage had earned him a place of honour amongst the world's master spies - a distinction rarely achieved by an agent during his own lifetime. Although he was fairly advanced in age, his enviable physique, remarkable vigour, and grim determination could put many a youthful colleague to shame. These attributes, combined with his rich and varied experience, prompted his government to defer his superannuation and post him to Turkey to another challenging assignment of far-reaching political importance.

Designated as 0X-13 within the intelligence set-up of his own country, he was given the cover name of Richard Welling for the duration of his latest assignment.

Richard Welling had a great flair for learning foreign languages. Before taking up a job in any foreign country, he always made it a point to master the local language. He thought this to be a great help in the discharge of his duties. It did not take him long to acquire a working knowledge of the Turkish language before embarking upon his new job. However, the delicate nature of his present mission necessitated a superlative mastery of the language so that he could go about as a Turk. The day he came across the maxim: "The best way to master a language is to have a longhaired dictionary," he decided to marry a Turkish lady. He did find one but his would-be in-laws insisted that Richard should embrace Islam before marriage. For a person like Richard Welling, religion had no connotation except devotion to duty. Professional expediency could overnight convert him to any religion. He therefore readily agreed to become a Muslim, little realising the physical implications involved. The bride's father demanded that the groom must undergo circumcision in token of having embraced Islam. It now dawned on Richard, that for a man (as opposed to a woman), it was not as easy to become a Muslim as becoming, for example, a Buddhist or a Christian. The very idea of undergoing that painful experience, especially at such an advanced stage in one's life, was terrifying. However, his professional devotion of a lifetime forced him to make a personal sacrifice, and he finally agreed to be circumcised. The rituals over, Richard Welling became Rashid Vali, the Muslim husband of a Turkish lady. All was now set for him to start his actual mission in Turkey. As always, he was hundred percent confident of success.

It sometimes happens that certain events cause a sudden and complete metamorphosis in the attitudes of an individual. Such a phenomenon took place in the case of Rashid Vali too, and the event responsible for this change was his conversion to Islam and his marriage to a Turkish lady. As a consequence of these events, he got an opportunity of coming into more intimate contact with the Turks. The more he saw of these people from such close quarters, the more he was convinced of their sincerity and selflessness, and their greatness as human beings. Spying against such fine people started pricking his conscience, although the voice of his conscience had been completely silenced by forty long years of surreptitious activities, often involving ruthlessness against innocent people. For the first time in his long career, this celebrated agent started feeling remorseful. And soon, a day came when he finally decided to go to the Turkish counter-intelligence department, disclose his actual identity and the nature of his assigned mission, pledge to give up spying for ever, and lead a happy life with his affectionate wife, living permanently amongst wonderful Turks.

Having made up his mind to surrender, Rashid landed up in the building that housed the Turkish counter-intelligence department. Moving through a labyrinth of long, tortuous corridors, he started visualising the likely reaction of the Turkish officials. "May be, they will arrest me straightaway," he thought. "Or perhaps they may subject me to prolonged interrogation to ascertain my antecedents." The possibility of physical torture also crossed his mind but that did not deter him from his decision to confess.

He knocked at one of the doors on the first floor and went in. The official across the table enquired about the object of his visit.

As Rashid wanted to make the whole affair short and snappy, he confessed everything in one go, including the name of the country for whom he had been operating in Turkey. For the official concerned, the name of "that country" was so awe-inspiring that he completely forgot that part of the story which concerned spying.

Seeing no signs of surprise on the official's face, Rashid repeated the name of "that country" for his benefit. The official jumped on his feet and extended his arm for a handshake saying: "Sir, I'm pleased to meet you. Please have a seat, sir!"

Yes, Rashid had not been wrong in his assessment of these fine people. Surely, they were so kind-hearted, otherwise why should they greet a foreign agent with a smile and a hand-shake, and offer him a seat in a government office? He took the chair. The official offered him a cigarette. Rashid Vali continued:

"I was saying, my real name is Richard Welling and I am known as agent 0X-13." The official told him his own name and appointment and then asked:

"What can we do for you, sir?"

This question startled Rashid, who had been expecting that the official would be taken aback on hearing his disclosures. Thinking that the official had probably not understood him, he repeated:

"I am a spy, an agent."

"Very good," replied the official. And then after musing for a while, he asked again:

"Can we do something for you?"

Before Rashid could answer that question, the official got up from his seat, patted the agent's shoulder and suggested:

"I think you should go to room 238 on the second floor and contact Mr. ... who is the official really concerned with this subject."

Rashid went to room 238 on the second floor and repeated all about himself and his assignment as a spy. The official concerned very seriously asked him:

"What type of spy are you? I mean what are the specific fields in which you do spying?"

"I am expert in sabotage, with specialty in the use of explosives for that purpose," replied Rashid.

"We have no vacancy in that branch," apologised the officer. "As a matter of fact, we are already surplus to establishment. I'm sorry, we won't be able to give you a job."

This was enough to irritate even a person like Rashid whose nerves had been abnormally strengthened by decades of spying. Raising his voice, he said:

"Look, I am telling you that I am a spy!"

"You may be right," replied the official very calmly, "but what can we do with you? Do you mean we should accord you special preferential treatment merely because you happen to be a spy?"

"I say, I am a secret agent," emphasised Rashid. "Is there nobody here who could take a little more interest in me? I assure you I could give you all the secret plans I have."

"I see," responded the official. "In that case, I hope you won't mind climbing up to the third floor. There, right at the end of the corridor, in the last room on the left, you shall find the right officer who deals with all matters concerning explosives."

And Rashid climbed up to the third floor and was soon standing in front of the official concerned:

"Sir, I am a spy," he announced.

The official was busy reading a newspaper. Without caring to raise his head, he asked the intruder: "Who has sent you to me?"

"I've come on my own."

"I mean, have you got a recommendatory letter from someone?"

"No, I've been directed to you by an officer in room 238. He said you deal with all matters connected with explosives."

"That's right, but what type of explosives?"

"For example those used for blowing up bridges."

"Did you say bridges?"

"Yes."

"Well, they have directed you to the wrong place, I'm afraid. We do deal with sabotage but not with sabotage of bridges."

"Alright, then whom should I contact?"

In order to gain a little extra time to think, the official started sucking one end of his pen. He then muttered:

"Bridges... bridges... bridges! O, yes. Please go up to the fourth floor and ask for the official dealing with the sabotage of bridges."

"Will someone on the fourth floor know who is the man concerned with this subject?" enquired Rashid.

"Sure. Ask anybody and they'll guide you."

The celebrated spy did as he was told. He found the man he was looking for, explained to him that he was a secret agent sent to Turkey for sabotage and for blowing up some important bridges, using explosives. After a patient hearing, the man asked him:

"What type of bridges, sir?"

Rashid was about to explode with rage, but exercising restraint, he replied:

"Just normal bridges."

Thinking he had not made his question very clear, the officer elucidated:

"I mean wooden bridges or concrete bridges; steel bridges or stone bridges; foot bridges, suspension bridges, or railway bridges? You know we have separate agencies dealing with different types of bridges."

"My specialisation is primarily steel bridges," replied Rashid.

"Ha! Why didn't you say so before? I'm afraid you are at the wrong place. If you don't mind, please go to room 601 on the sixth floor and there you'll find the proper person to attend to your problem. And do give him my regards."

A little more hopeful this time, Rashid climbed to the sixth floor and found room 601. He repeated everything from A to Z. The official there appeared deeply engrossed. Rashid thought he must be working out the course of action to follow when, as if suddenly reminded of something more important, the man dialled his telephone and said:

"Sir, a gentleman is here with me. He claims to be a spy entrusted with sabotage, mostly by blowing up steel bridges using high explosive. What are your orders for him, sir?"

Rashid was now sure that he would be arrested immediately and subjected to severe interrogation. He was waiting in great suspense when the man replaced the telephone handset with his last sentence:

"As you order, sir." And then, turning to Rashid, he said:

"Sir, the director has advised that you go to Mr. Hashmi on the top floor, and he would do what is needed."

Rashid complied. He narrated everything to Mr. Hashmi on the top floor. The latter asked him:

"How do you ignite the explosive used for blowing up bridges?" With his face turned red with rage, Rashid shouted:

"Whatever method I employ to ignite the explosives, does that in any manner concern you?"

Mr. Hashmi tried to pacify Rashid with his soft voice:

"Please don't get annoyed. You claim to be a spy and yet you get irritated at nothing. You should know that irritable persons can never make good spies. I had asked this question only to facilitate your own job. You see, the selection dealing with the blowing up of steel bridges with ignition fuses is different from the one that blows them up electrically. Both these techniques are different and they need different specialists."

Thoroughly disgusted, Rashid replied:

"I sometimes use fuses and sometimes electricity for igniting the explosive. Please let it be known that I am a spy, a saboteur, an enemy agent! Isn't that enough?"

"Why didn't you say so earlier? I'm afraid you'll have to go down to the first floor and contact the official who sits in the third room on the right."

Rashid descended to the first floor and entered the third room on the right. With a last hope, he again narrated everything from beginning to end. The official who had already put on his overcoat impatiently looked at his watch and, with a frowning face, said:

"That's fine, sir, but why have you come here so late? The working hours are about to finish. The office will be closed very soon. Your case is important as well as time-consuming."

Rashid explained that he was late because for the whole day he had been going from floor to floor and room to room in the same building to find the appropriate person. The official, raising his voice gradually as he spoke, said:

"I understand, I understand. But whatever the case, why couldn't you come here early in the morning? Why should one come here just when the office is about to close?"

"But," Rashid was about to say something when the official, raising his hand in disgust, interrupted him:

"Please come tomorrow morning, and come early."

On his way back from the counter-intelligence department that evening, Rashid was engrossed in deep thoughts. He reluctantly arrived at the conclusion that, whether one likes it or not, one has no option but to continue spying in that great country called Turkey. He was soon back to his assigned job as Agent 0X-13.

Human Offspring

Papa ant and Mama ant gathered their offspring to give them a lesson on "antship". Papa ant rounded off the lesson thus:

"My children! Always try to be an ant in life. Never leave the path of antship."

"But how can we become real ants? What are the methods to be followed?" they asked.

"Take us as your models," replied Papa ant, "and go on doing what we do."

The offspring closely watched their parents and always did what their parents did. As summer began, they collected bits and pieces of eatables and stocked these underground. When winter came, they slept through it. As the appropriate time approached, they laid eggs. One day, Papa ant and Mama ant again collected their offspring.

"My dear children," said Papa ant, "I am about to die. I am very happy with you all. I am glad you have all become ants at last. None of you ever departed from the true path of antship. May God be pleased with you."

*

Papa fish and Mama fish gathered their offspring to give them a lesson on how to become real fish. Papa fish rounded off the lesson thus:

"My kids! Always try to be a fish in life. Never leave the path of fishiness."

"But how can we become real fish, Papa?" they enquired. "Tell us the ways to become good fish."

"Take the two of us as your models and keep doing whatever we do," replied Papa fish.

So the fish offspring kept watching their parents and always did what their parents did. They swam in the sea; devoured smaller fish; some getting devoured by the big fish. They laid eggs and multiplied as their parents had been multiplying. One day, Papa fish and Mama fish called their offspring and the former talked to them thus:

"My dear kids! At last you are all grown up. You have all become real nice fish. You never deviated from the path of fishiness. It means our effort did not go waste. We can both die in peace now. May God be pleased with you."

"We couldn't do much, Papa," said the offspring. "We only did what you and Mama did in life."

*

Papa duck and Mama duck gathered their offspring and gave them a lesson on being good ducks in life. Papa duck said to them:

"My children! Try to be good ducks in life. Never leave the path of duckship."

"What should we do to become good ducks, Papa?" asked the duck offspring.

"That's very simple," replied Papa duck. "Make us your models and just do whatever we two do."

So the offspring kept watching their parents and always did whatever their parents did. They learnt how to do "quack quack". They swam in water and walked on land. They picked up their mates, laid eggs, hatched these and produced their own offspring. One day, Papa duck and Mama duck again called their offspring and the former talked to them thus:

"My dear kids! At last you are all full-bloomed ducks. Each one of you has become a good duck. None of you deviated from the path of duckship. Our efforts in bringing you up have not been in vain. May God be pleased with you."

*

Papa dog and Mama dog also gathered their offspring one day and started giving them a lesson on "dogship." Papa dog rounded off the lesson thus:

"My children! Try to be good dogs in life. Never deviate from the path of dogship."

"What should we do to become good dogs. Papa?" asked the little pups.

"That's quite simple," replied Papa dog. "Just take me and your Mama as models and keep doing whatever we two do."

So the little pups kept watching their parents and did whatever the Papa dog and Mama dog did. They barked and they performed watchdog duties. They learnt to be faithful to the master. Then they picked up their mates and multiplied as their parents had been multiplying. One day, Papa dog and Mama dog again called their offspring and this is how the former addressed them:

"My dear kids! You are all grown up now. Every one of you has become a good dog. None of you deviated from the path of dogship. We are glad our efforts to bring you up did not go waste. May God be pleased with you all."

*

Camels, oxen, elephants, sheep, snakes, in short all creatures born as males and females told their offspring to copy them and keep doing what they themselves did. Their offspring also followed them, doing whatever the parents did. And in the end all the offspring became good specimens of their respective species. Before breathing their last, the parents of these offspring told them how happy they were to see their young ones having come up to their expectations.

*

Papa man and Mama man also called their offspring and started giving them a lesson on how to become good human beings. Papa man rounded off the lesson in these words:

"My dear children! In life always try to be good human beings. Never deviate from the path of humanity."

"But how can we become true human beings?" asked the children of man. What should we do for becoming good human beings?"

"That's very simple," replied Papa man. "Take me and your mama as your models and always do whatever we two do."

So the offspring of man watched Papa man and Mama man and they all did whatever their parents did. As a result, they became hundred percent true likes of their Papa and Mama. One day, Papa man and Mama man gathered their children and this is what Papa man had to tell them:

"It's a shame!" he shouted at them. "None of you has come up to our expectations. Your upbringing has been a miserable failure. None of you has been able to become a human being. You are all miles away from the standards of humanity. As a matter of fact, you have given up everything characteristic of human beings. It is now time for us to go to the next world. What a pity, all our efforts to bring you up in a befitting manner have gone waste. May God damn you all!!"

The offspring of man were utterly bewildered.

"OK Papa, but why are you cursing us?" they asked in amazement. "Have we done something wrong?.. We have done nothing but what you yourself have been doing all your life. It was you whom we took as our model at all times... Is it then we who are to blame for what we are today?"

Chains and Shadows

Sometime in history, there existed a country which no longer appears in any book of geography. As the legend goes, the physical appearance of the people of that country suddenly started undergoing major changes.

At first their heads started suppressing their shoulders, so much so that pretty soon their necks almost disappeared. Then everybody's back started bending, with the result that the whole nation became a nation of hunchbacks. Ultimately, it became difficult for people to lift their feet off the ground to walk properly. They had to drag along to go from place to place. It seemed as if the entire population was constantly under some invisible pressure, with heavy chains shackled to their ankles. Fairly soon, young and old, men and women, started groaning. The two most frequently heard sentences on their lips were:

"Oh, we cannot pull it now!"

"Oof, we cannot bear it now!"

Gradually, their voices turned into wailing. It was only when the people's groans and wails reached the seventh heaven, that the ruler of the day also happened to hear the cries of woe. Annoyed, he asked his courtiers:

"Where are these detestable sounds coming from? They are disturbing our sweet slumber."

The courtiers replied:

"Your Majesty! These are the cries of your subjects for help. In the beginning, when these sounds hit our ears, we took these as the hissing of the wind. That hissing soon turned into buzzing, but we still paid no heed. And when the buzzing turned into din, we plugged our ears with our fingers in an effort to block out the noise. If your Majesty permits, we may cut off some vocal chords of every individual, so that people's loud cries may not disturb Your Honour's sleep."

The ruler of the day admonished the courtiers:

"We are living in modern times, not in medieval ages. Don't talk of yesterday, for the moment today begins, yesterday is buried. Instead of suggesting to us a miserably outdated remedy, let it be announced throughout the country, for all our subjects to gather in the capital's main square, so that my Majesty may address them as per modern tradition."

The next day, when people gathered in the main square, the ruler for the first time noticed their hunched backs and heads perched directly on their neck-less shoulders. Surprised, he asked sympathetically:

"What is bothering you people?"

"We cannot pull it now!"

"We cannot bear it now!"

The ruler asked a few top brains from amongst the audience to come forward.

"Tell me the truth," he said. "What is it that all of you cannot pull? And what is it that you can't bear?"

"Your Majesty! We are ourselves at a loss to say what exactly is wrong. It seems as if we have been chained to fetters whose unbearable weight prevents us from walking in the normal manner. These mysterious chains are becoming heavier and heavier every day. If this process continues, pretty soon the whole nation will come to a standstill. Men will become nailed to earth and look no different from trees. Your Majesty! These chains have become so heavy that we have no more strength to pull them along."

The ruler smiled:

"I see! So that's why my people cannot pull. But you folks keep repeating another slogan too. What's it that you cannot bear?"

"Your Majesty! We feel as if a mysterious load has been placed on our heads. Like the chains, this load has also been increasing day by day. As a result, our necks have completely vanished. Your Honour! We can no longer bear this load."

On this the ruler addressed his people:

"My dear countrymen! You don't have to worry at all. This very day, we are going to appoint a committee of the most capable of our experts to determine the nature of the mysterious chains that bind you and the load that bothers you. As soon as the committee's report is received, you will once again become fit enough to carry your usual loads and to pull your normal chains."

This brightened up the people's faces. Dragging their feet, they all dispersed to their homes.

That very day, the ruler picked up forty of his official experts and said to them:

"His Majesty is sure you people are also aware of the problems confronting our subjects. It was to meet such extraordinary challenges that you people have been brought up and fed for years at end, at a very heavy cost. Time has now come when you should pay back at least partially, for the favours done to you. We want you to find out the exact nature of the strange load that our people can no longer bear. You should propose some solution to reduce that load. However, beware not to suggest anything that may irritate my Majesty. After all, safeguarding my Majesty's rights is also your foremost duty. Use the power of your knowledge and intellect to find out a solution, just the one I want, to stop the shouting and crying of our subjects."

The experts replied:

"Your Majesty's orders shall be obeyed. We have just one request to make. We want a period of forty days during which we should be fed on forty bags of almonds and sultana, so that our brains become sufficiently enlightened. Right on the forty-first day, we shall present a solution in keeping with your Majesty's desires, for determining the nature of the people's load and reducing its weight."

While accepting this condition, the ruler warned the experts again:

"Remember, if your proposal goes against my interests, I shall cut you into two each and make eighty experts out of you forty."

To prevent them from wasting their time, the ruler had the experts locked up in a big room of his palace. A bag of almonds and sultanas was pushed into the room daily and the door locked again.

While the experts were having a jolly time in the room, feeding themselves on almonds and sultanas, the groans and wails of the masses once again started reaching the ruler's ears. Perturbed by the noise, he would peep into the experts' room through the key-hole and always see them doing nothing but relishing their daily feed, or having had their feed, jumping and skipping around. He would grind his teeth in anger, saying to himself:

"You rascals! Let the period of forty days end, and if you utter a single word against my interests, I shall chop you into dog feed. Let me renounce my kingship if I don't do that."

On the forty-first day, the king ordered the experts out of the locked room. The most expert amongst them addressed the ruler:

"Your Majesty! After untiring labour and mental exercise, we have been able to determine the nature of the people's problems. Our research shows that the mysterious load bothering our countrymen is nothing but the weight of their own shadows. These shadows do not leave them alone, and remain clinging all the time to their feet. The more the shadows pull them towards the earth, the heavier the load they feel on their backs. This is the load under which your Majesty's subjects find themselves being crushed."

The ruler was very happy to hear this diagnosis. He showered praises on the experts' knowledge and intellect, and ordered that their opinion be conveyed to the masses immediately, that the people be advised to find ways and means of getting rid of their shadows, and somehow learn to live without these, if they wanted to be rid of their mysterious load.

The royal decree was conveyed to the people without delay. The people's faces brightened up once again. From that very day, an unending war between man and man's shadow started. People would run very fast to get rid of their shadows, ultimately dropping down dead tired. On getting up on their feet, they would find the shadow still clinging to them. Despite their best efforts, nobody could run fast enough to outdistance his shadow.

People even used horse carriages and chariots to run away to places far off from their shadows but the moment they arrived at the destination, they would find the shadows stuck to their feet. At dawn, they would find the shadows in the west and would therefore run away to the east. The race towards the east would continue till midday, when their shadows would start leading them, forcing them to run westward, leaving the shadows in the east.

In that nation of people running all the time like fools, from east to west and west to east, there appeared some leaders who would address the masses every morning:

"Dear countrymen! Our salvation lies in the East. Let us turn towards the East and run all together."

Impressed by the apparent sincerity of these leaders, people would start running Eastwards. After midday, another set of leaders would surround the masses and deliver speeches:

"Brothers! Our salvation lies in the West. Let us all run Westward."

Following their leaders' advice, the poor masses ran now to the East, now to the West, but nobody could escape from his shadow, nor did anybody's load decrease.

The contradictory advice of leaders became more and more vociferous, leading to bitter arguments between them every morning, midday, and evening.

When long speeches for salvation in the East or the West could not solve the people's problems, a third group of leaders jumped into the arena, with a new piece of advice.

"Comrades!" they said. "Those who show you the garden path to the East or the West are traitors. Take our advice and run neither to the East nor to the West, but stay in the centre."

People now started following this advice. Their shadows became smaller and smaller on the approach of midday. This made them shout in joy:

"Ahha! We are just about to get rid of these wretched things."

But their joy never proved long-lasting. As soon as the midday was over, shadows again started lengthening. When nobody could escape from his shadow, the supporters of the three political groups started indulging in frequent physical duels. Disgusted of this recurring nuisance, the people started shouting and groaning again:

"Oh! We cannot pull it now."

"Off. We cannot bear it now."

Echoed by the parapets of the royal palace, the groans reached the ruler's ears. Greatly perturbed, he shouted:

"What's all this pandemonium that is disturbing our sleep again?" The courtiers replied:

"Your Majesty! This is the voice of your subjects who have not been able to get rid of their shadows, no matter whether they ran to the East or to the West, or kept standing still in the middle."

The ruler again gathered his forty experts and shouted in rage:

"Did I bring you up for years so that you don't come to my aid in the hour of my need? Today my Majesty will give you folks the last chance to demonstrate the power of your expertise. All of you join heads and find out a way by which our beloved subjects may get permanent riddance from their shadows so that their lips may emit no more groans to disturb our peaceful sleep."

The experts repeated the same old conditions to which the ruler agreed. They were locked in a room for forty days and were fed on almonds and sultanas as before. They were taken out on the forty-first day when the top-most expert addressed the ruler:

"Your Majesty! A feed of almonds and sultanas for forty days has illuminated our brains to an extent that we have found a method, absolutely in accordance with the wishes of your Honour, to enable your subjects to get rid of their shadows."

"Let the method be explained," ordained the ruler. The top-most expert complied:

"Your Majesty! You know that shadows disappear automatically when it gets dark. Hence, in our humble opinion, to save the people from their shadows, it is necessary to create permanent darkness of night throughout the country."

The ruler went furious.

"But you wretched fellows, how will you create the darkness of night during daylight?" he asked.

"Your Majesty! We shall have the daylight dyed in darkness. For that, all your Honour needs is a dungeon into which the entry of even a single ray of sunlight should be made impossible. Whoever dares open his lips to protest and disturb Your Majesty's peace, shall be thrown into the dungeon. And with that, his shadow will also disappear. Freed of the weight of his shadow, he will stop shouting and crying."

Accordingly, the ruler had a dungeon built. To prevent sunlight from getting in, not even the smallest hole was left open. Whosoever was seen raising a cry of protest was picked up and thrown into the dungeon. As soon as his shadow disappeared, leave alone his cries, nobody ever heard even his normal voice. In this way, those inside the dungeon were saved from their shadows. However, those still outside, continued groaning from morning till evening. How many persons could be shoved into the dungeon anyway? Before long, it was full to an inch. The ruler had it expanded. Fairly soon, it became over-crowded again and was again expanded. This process continued till the whole country was converted into a vast dungeon. Sunlight could penetrate only a few selected spots in the country, where the ruler and his family, the royal staff, the courtiers, and the special experts lived, along with millions of shadows of those who had been thrown into the dungeon. These shadows could not be seen at night, but as soon as the day broke, they started crawling on the ground. Having played the role of human shadows for ages and spent years in the company of man, these shadows now looked just like human beings. However, they could not stand on their own feet as men do. In addition, some odd members of the public were also still outside the dungeon, but the fear of the dungeon had made them lock their own lips.

Nobody had the courage to say:

"We cannot pull it," or

"We cannot bear it."

On the contrary, they were heard saying voluntarily:

"We are now quite used to it. We can now pull it, and we can bear it too."

Thereafter, the groans and cries of woe of the subjects never reached the ears of the ruler of that country, nor was his sleep ever disturbed.

The Cost of a Sensational Find

Followed by a crowd of junior doctors and medical students, the Professor entered the Eye Department and went into one of the wards. This Professor in-charge of the Eye Department had the reputation of being highly peevish, reticent and harsh. He seldom smiled. His fragile attitude made him scatter-brained and offish all around. He looked more like a First World War type of general than a man belonging to the medical profession. Not only his students but also his friends used to keep at a safe distance from him. However, in his own field he had earned world-wide fame. He was a member of quite a few international medical societies and associations. His discoveries and learned writings were given a place of prestige in international medical magazines. That is why he was accorded due respect by everybody.

While on a round of the wards, the Professor used to stop in front of each patient for not more than a minute. The accompanying doctors and students used to remain fairly uneasy throughout the daily round for fear of being asked a question of which they might not know the right answer.

"Is this a new patient?" he asked.

"Yes Sir," replied an assistant doctor. "He came yesterday."

"What's the problem with him?"

"We have not yet been able to diagnose it, Sir. He complains of severe pain in both his eyes and has constant headache."

The Professor gazed at the painful eyes of the patient from a distance and, hardly opening his mouth, uttered in an almost inaudible voice:

"Tests?"

"Have been carried out, Sir."

"Pus."

A man of very few words, the Professor ordered a pus test to be carried out, and then left the ward. Those accompanying him were mighty happy that the daily round had gone off very well that day.

Two assistant doctors took a pus swab from the eyes of the patient and brought it to the professor in his room. The latter kept gazing into the microscope for a long time. When he removed his eyes from the microscope for a moment, a smile could be discerned on his face. This was a rare event for the two doctors who had been working with him for a long time. The Professor later picked up a few voluminous books from the book-shelf and started turning their pages one by one. In the process, he would mutter such words and phrases as:

"That's it!"... "I see"... "Aha!" etc.

After some time he looked at the two assistant doctors waiting keenly in the room: "Call the other doctors as well," he said. "Let the students also join in."

Pretty soon, the Professor's room was full of young doctors and a host of students.

The Professor seemed to be in an unusually festive mood, like a small child of a poor family who had received an unexpectedly precious gift. One could see this serious gentleman moving about the microscope with joy.

"Gentlemen! We are lucky. Very lucky, indeed," he said. "We have in front of us a very rare microbe. There are today many eye specialists who have never witnessed an event of this nature in their whole life. How lucky for you to be seeing this thing while you are students or young doctors. You come across this disease in not one patient out of a million, rather one out of ten or even fifteen million."

The Professor's joy and enthusiasm could be gauged from the way he was rubbing his hands against each other and the frequency with which he was repeating his remarks: "A very rare microbe."

"In my own life, this is the second time that I have seen this rare microbe," he continued. "It was as a student in Paris that my teacher showed it to me for the first time. The patient was an African. You know, if this disease is not treated within forty-eight hours of the entry of the microbe into a patient's eyes, he is bound to become blind. With that, his pain completely disappears. Hence, it is very important that treatment should start at once."

Turning to one of the doctors, he asked:

"When did the patient start having pain?"

"Since yesterday morning, Sir. He was hospitalised last night."

"This means if we don't intervene, he will be a blind man after another 24 hours. You know, the pain is really dreadful. This is because once the microbe settles down in the secretive glands it starts multiplying at a tremendous rate, ultimately reaching the centre of vision in the brain, thereby permanently impairing the patient's eye-sight. Now I want all of you to come to the microscope one by one and examine this rare microbe very minutely."

While the doctors and the students went through this exercise, the Professor kept constantly telephoning his friends in the medical profession, giving them the good news about this rare species. His extreme excitement was clear indication of the extent to which he was devoted to his profession. His conversation on the telephone ran something like this:

"My dear Sir, this is really something tremendous... It is not an event that you come across every now and then... So it means you too have never seen it before... I don't think any other doctor in this country has seen it either... We are lucky indeed... I am terribly excited you know..."

In between his telephone calls, he would give instructions to the students and explain certain details about the disease:

"This microbe cannot survive in open air. When exposed, it dies at once. That's why the disease is not infectious. Otherwise the whole mankind could turn blind because of this microbe. Please make sure you handle it very carefully."

The Professor was guarding the microbe the way one would guard one's most precious possession. In the excitement of things, he even forgot his mid-day meal. He assigned different tasks to the doctors and the students in connection with his new find. Two of them were to prepare a thousand-time enlargement of a colour picture of the microbe. One of the doctors, with the help of a few students, was to prepare culture for the multiplication of the rare species. And so on. He himself got engrossed in some books to prepare his own notes for a lecture he intended to deliver on the subject.

That day, no work other than that connected with the new find was done in the Eye Department. Doctors, nurses and even the maids kept themselves busy with the new subject. Such great hustle and bustle had never been witnessed in the hospital before. The whole atmosphere was humming with activity. Doctors from other departments of the hospital, specialists from other hospitals and many friends of the Professor from private hospitals had by now rushed to the Eye Department where the Professor was busy describing the event almost non-stop. Unlike the normal practice, work continued till late that evening. Preparations continued for the Professor's lecture scheduled for the next morning in the faculty lecture hall.

The Professor went home very late. There too, he continued with his lecture notes. It was going to occupy a very important place in the medical literature of the world. He hardly slept that night. Even when asleep, he continued struggling with the rare microbe. Next morning he dashed to the hospital unusually early. He was worried. Did the microbe survive overnight? For him the most important thing on earth was how to make it survive and multiply outside the secretive gland of a human being. On arrival, he was thrilled to find the microbes very much living and multiplying in the culture that his assistants had prepared according to his instructions.

A large but select audience attended the lecture. After the lecture, the Professor sent a large number of telegrams to his old colleagues and teachers in other countries, giving them the sensational news. In the meantime, some doctors observed that the microbe which was originally round and circular in shape would become thinner and longer before splitting into two. They rushed to the Professor's room to give him this new information. So excited were they, that they forgot to knock at the door before entering. They were stunned to find the Professor, along with some of his friends, dancing and singing with joy! On hearing about the new phenomenon, he directed the assistant doctors to gather everybody in his room. He also disclosed his intention of writing a book on the subject very soon. And then all of a sudden he was reminded of the patient. "How is the patient?" he enquired.

"His pain has stopped completely, Sir," replied the doctor in charge.

"This means?.."

"He can't see any longer, Sir."

The Professor gave a grinning smile and exclaimed: "You see! I told you folks. If the patient is not treated for 48 hours, he is bound to lose his eyesight. As his pain had started the day before yesterday, he should have lost his sight this morning, no intervention having been made. Wasn't I right?"

"That's right, Sir," agreed the assistants.

"My lads, science never makes mistakes... I had told you everything."

The Professor, along with the assistant doctors and the medical students were all back in the Eye Department to carry on with the research on the world's rarest microbe. They were all still full of joy and enthusiasm!

Corruption Unlimited

As I have no secrets to hide from you, let me confess that although my pay was just a thousand Liras, I was living in a house whose monthly rent was twelve hundred. The same was more or less true of all my colleagues. The source of our extra earning was fully known to the high-ups but nobody could ever manage to plug it. It won't be wrong to say that the very nature of our job was such that it left us with no option but to let additional money flow in. And mind you, we never indulged in swindling or fraud. No misappropriation of government funds, and no usurpation of anybody's legitimate rights. A magic sentence (YOUR BILL HAS NOT YET BEEN PASSED) was all that we uttered and every contractor would rush to grease our palms voluntarily.

Despite our frequent use of the above gold-minting formula, we were fair to all contractors and ensured that all bills were passed; of course some of these were passed forthwith while for others the contractors had to undertake dozens of trips to our exalted office before they got their payment. Our innocent manipulation with bills caused no loss to the state or to the contractors. As a matter of fact, the latter felt grateful to us because it was always with our ultimate cooperation that they could manage to retrieve heavy sums, which would otherwise keep rotting in government treasuries.

During the two years that I had been working in that office, my pockets were always bursting at the seams with money. My colleagues also rolled in wealth. We all used to wonder how bounteous nature had been to us. To us, this prosperity was a real miracle, especially when we realised that it was not at the cost of anybody else. Ours was more of a mint than a government office, and this mint was for the exclusive benefit of those who operated it.

Another interesting point: our business was all above board. No hush-hush, no underhand dealings. Contractors paid us openly and we openly shared each day's earnings amongst us. The division was done on a real fraternal basis, the elder brothers (occupying senior positions) receiving a bigger proportion than their junior younger brothers. The mutual relationship among the staff appeared to be identical to that which normally exists amongst the members of a joint stock company. However, while a joint stock company is governed by rules framed under an act of the legislature, our "company" had come into being on its own and had no written rules of business. In spite of the absence of any written bye-laws, no member ever dared point a finger at any of his colleagues, nor talk about the "company" affairs with any outside elements.

The distribution of "spoils" was done in a most fair manner, keeping all canons of justice in view. If a member of the staff happened to be absent on a particular day, his share used to be set aside and delivered to him with remarkable honesty the very next morning. Likewise, the share of those who proceeded on long leave was accounted for throughout their absence and the accumulated amount handed over to them the day they rejoined from leave.

Just as there was nothing secret about our transactions, there was nothing secret about the rates we charged. These were fixed on highly rational basis and were known to all of us. For contracts up to a value of one hundred thousand liras, our share was one and a half percent, rising to three percent for contracts above that value. The rate increased in direct proportion to the speed with which a bill was passed for payment. For example, if a bill was passed in ten days as against the normal twenty, our share was automatically doubled. The nature of each contract was also an important factor that determined our share. We charged relatively more in case of transport contracts and construction work. Our rates fluctuated in case of supply contracts, depending on the season and the prevailing market conditions. In short, the rates were so explicit and arithmetical in nature that as soon as a bill was passed, right from the boss down to the office attendants, everybody could accurately calculate his own share of the "booty" to the last penny. Under these circumstances it was simply impossible for any single individual to enter into collusion with a contractor and pocket the entire commission secretly, to the exclusion of all his colleagues. It is said that before my arrival in that office, some unscrupulous selfish fellows did try to indulge in this immoral practice, thereby depriving their colleagues of their legitimate share of extra earnings, but as soon as others got a wind of this, they established a powerful united front against those mean creatures. The united front was so strong and cohesive that it could well serve as a model for a country's dissident political parties. Unity being strength, as the popular saying goes, the united front managed to have the dirty fish amongst the staff arrested on charges of corruption, thereby saving the whole pond from being polluted by their obnoxious stench. The unhealthy practice was thus uprooted before it turned into a mean tradition. All members of the staff started realising that it would be foolish to strangle the hen that laid the golden egg, merely for the personal benefit of an odd avaricious individual.

Before joining that office, I had been working elsewhere for fifteen hundred a month. To get the new job (carrying less pay), I had not only to sacrifice a higher salary but had to bribe a very close friend of mine, four thousand net, plus a lifelong gratitude for his kind favour. My friend "sold" me his seat due to some personal compulsions which forced him to go to another station, otherwise who would like to part with a gold mine for a paltry sum of four thousand bucks? Whoever once got himself posted to that office, refused to leave for the rest of his life. Such was the attraction it offered. My friend was wise enough to make me promise to surrender the seat back to him without any fuss, in case his circumstances ever allowed him to come back. Many had offered him as much as twenty thousand for his seat but he refused. He was afraid that the higher bidder may prove unreliable and may not vacate in his favour if and when he decided to return. As he had full confidence in me, his old friend, and was keen to oblige me, he decided in my favour at a real throw-away price of four thousand.

As soon as I reported for duty, a chain of visible changes for the better started taking place in my family. My wife and children started putting on weight. My wife who had not gained even a gram over the previous twenty years was becoming two kilos heavier every twenty days. Huge lumps of flesh could be seen protruding at her hips, buttocks, and paunch. I became worried about the extent to which she was going to expand before putting on brakes. As for myself, all my trousers became unbearably tight at the waist and had to be discarded in favour of new ones.

Our living standard improved so fast that even a casual observer could not miss the change. Just as my tummy had started feeling uneasy in my trousers, the members of my family started feeling suffocated in our old house. Our daughter had remained unmarried in spite of her unlimited character qualities and our untiring efforts for many long years. The burden of advancing age had caused discoloring of her once beautiful face. Once again her old charm came back and she started looking prettier than the moon. We revived our efforts to find her a suitable match and pretty soon there was a bee-line of candidates.

We were living a highly enjoyable life when a man called Haider landed up in our office. Nobody knew who was instrumental in his posting to us. His arrival spoiled the sport. The boss sent him to work in the transport section. He was lean and thin, with hardly any flesh on his body. Every new-comer used to be physically as emaciated as Haider on first joining our set-up. We therefore thought it won't be long before Haider too became healthy, plump, and cheerful like us. We were wrong. Haider became weaker and weaker as the days passed. If you saw him taking his usual long strides, you would have mistaken him for a dead man's reincarnated skeleton.

The day after Haider's arrival, our boss held a staff meeting to decide about the quantum of Haider's share. After prolonged discussion, it was agreed to pay him forty six Liras for that day as the day's income had been rather less than normal. The task of delivering the amount to Haider was entrusted to me. I went to him when the office closed. After exchange of salutations, I placed the envelope containing his share on his table.

"What's this?" he enquired.

"This is your share of today's income."

"What income? What share?"

I grinned in reply, as is normally done on such occasions. With the back of his hand, Haider threw the envelope on the ground.

"I do NOT want any share," he snarled.

I quietly picked up the envelope and went to narrate the story to the boss.

"This stupid fellow looks like an honest person. What a misfortune," he remarked on hearing me.

A craftier colleague advised the boss:

"Sir, he might have returned the money for being inadequate. This is one way of putting higher premium on oneself."

Haider's share was unanimously increased. Another gentleman was deputed to deliver it to him the next day. The new representative apologetically explained to Haider:

"We are sorry there was some mix-up yesterday. The money sent to you was less than your due share. The actual decision about your share was that you would be paid more than what any other person of your status is being paid. I have today brought you your full share for yesterday as well as today."

Haider chased out that worthy delegate also.

We knew a single dissident could create problems for all of us. All of us were therefore keen somehow to entice Haider to become a co-sharer so that he may not have the guts to deprive everybody else of their livelihood.

For a whole week, nobody dared accept a single penny from any contractor for fear of Haider. If things were allowed to go on like that, we were afraid our families would soon start losing weight once again. If one has always remained emaciated, one gets used to it; but having had the taste of sound health and a plump body, reversion to poor health can result in immense mental complications. We prayed to God to save us from such an eventuality.

All our efforts to bring Haider to the "right" path through persuasion proved futile. He continued coming to office every morning, taking his usual ghost-like strides, and going back in the afternoon, as unsoiled, as unpolluted as ever. The accursed fellow had a blank, expressionless face, indicating complete disregard of everybody else working around him. It appeared he never considered any one of us as human beings.

There was a lurking fear amongst us all, that Haider had been deliberately planted amongst us so that the higher authorities could be kept informed of our activities. Very soon, this fear turned from a mere suspicion to a firm belief. This gave accelerated impetus to our efforts to convert Haider, so much so that a contractor was sent to lure him into accepting the entire commission of his bill without the knowledge of others. The contractor was back on his heels:

"This fellow is a real rascal," he reported. "I tried hard but could not make him accept the proposal. If I had stayed any longer, he was going to get me handcuffed. Never have I come across a more discourteous man in my life."

One day, a person named Jalil came to our office and said:

"If you give me a job, I can rid you of that abominable absurdity called Haider."

Jalil's proposal was accepted at once. He haggled a lot about his terms of service. It was finally decided that if Jalil succeeded in chasing out Haider, he would be absorbed against a janitor's vacancy on a monthly pay of Liras fifty; however, his share of the daily extra income would be no less than that of the boss himself.

After a few days, the Director General and two senior officers from our Head Office came for our annual inspection. The staff hosted a lunch in their honour in the canteen. Haider was sitting aloof on a table, his eyebrows raised and his face pulled long as usual. When coffee was being served, Jalil entered the hall, ran excitedly towards Haider, hugged him as hard as he could, and shouted:

"Hello, Haider dear." Haider looked flabbergasted.

"Excuse me, but I have not been able to place you," he apologised.

"Come on now, Haider, my brother! Don't try to be clever," said Jalil.

"My dear sir, I have honestly not been able to recognise you," reasserted Haider.

Their dialogue had drawn everybody's attention. Jalil raised his voice further:

"Look here! Don't you remember the days when we used to visit Ankara's out of bound areas together? Never mind, forget about that. But I'm sure you haven't forgotten the long rigorous imprisonment to which you were sentenced for defrauding a government department of God knows how many millions, and how the relentless efforts of my lawyer got you out of jail after just one year's imprisonment."

"That is utter nonsense," protested Haider. "You are certainly under some misunderstanding."

"Now don't try to befool me, Haider. I have absolutely no doubt that it was you who was later serving as a cashier in a bank from where you disappeared after misappropriating fifteen thousand Liras."

Mad with rage, Haider rolled up his sleeves in defence:

"Look here, mister! I do NOT recognise you and I do NOT know what you are talking about. I am sure this is a case of mistaken identities."

"Come, come, Haider!" repeated Jalil. "Let me refresh your memory in a minute. Don't you remember you had fallen victim to a dancer's web of intrigues, and had to indulge in still another case of fraud to find money for meeting her ever-increasing demands?"

"This is preposterous."

Jalil continued:

"What I say is hundred per cent correct. Can you also deny that incident when you were caught red-handed while accepting illegal gratification and your daughter had to go to the police station to..."

"Will you shut up your mouth!" roared Haider. "Whose daughter? What police station are you talking about?"

Jalil ignored Haider's harsh words and protestation. He continued with a smile:

"Now that's really a limit, Haider. It is the height of ingratitude refusing to recognise a man who used to visit you so frequently when you were in jail, who spent his own money to keep you constantly supplied with cigarettes, fruit, and a dozen other essential items for a period of one full year. I am sure you are kidding."

Absolutely red with anger, Haider got up from his seat and left the hall.

In the heart of their hearts, nobody present in the canteen was prepared to believe that Haider could have done whatever had just been attributed to him by Jalil. In spite of that, people exchanged meaningful glances, as if saying to each other:

"You see? What misdeeds these so-called virtuous people can commit! How shameless!"

Within two days of that incident, Haider was relieved of his job on receipt of orders from the Head Office. Jalil got the promised post of a janitor, with a pay of fifty Liras but at par with the boss in the sharing of our daily booty.

Beware of the Rats Amongst Us

Once upon a time... In one of the countries...

O no, this is not a cooked up fable... The right thing would be to narrate the event, giving the place and the time of its occurrence. The time was some time after the birth of Christ, and the place, somewhere on this earth.

Now that we have the time and place, let's go on to the narration.

At the above time and place, there used to be a huge depot. The depot was full to the brim, with eatables, items of clothing, detergents, firewood, etc. Everything had been stocked in proper order. You had rice, grams, beans and lentils on one side; wheat, barley, rye and oats on another side. Soap, oil and butter laid out in one section; shoes, clothing and apparel in another section.

The management of this depot was in the hands of a know-all. One day, this competent know-all was in a fix as to what to do, for the depot had been occupied by rats. The eatables were found dwindling day by day, more and more cakes of cheese were seen nibbled daily. Of course the competent manager did not sit idle, with hands folded across his chest. He fought a determined battle against the rats. But whatever he did, he could not win this battle. The nibbled lumps of cheese and soap cakes started completely disappearing as the days went by. The items of clothing turned into rags. Bags of flour became habitats of rats.

No place in the depot was safe from the intruders. As the rodents nourished themselves on grain and butter, they became fatter and fatter. As they grew in size, they became more and more unmanageable and their breeding rate increased further. Pretty soon, the huge depot was virtually under the occupation of an army of rats. It was no longer possible to deal with them. They did not remain content with devouring the eatables and nibbling at clothing, but also started sharpening their teeth on shoes, leather sheets and even on wooden stuff.

Ultimately, they nourished themselves into cat-size rats, reaching the size of dogs in no time. There was no obstacle for them in the depot now. They could run around and play hide and seek at will. The worst part of the game was that even the most sunny and beautiful parts of the depot also went under their occupation very soon.

The competent manager continued the war against the rodents undeterred. He placed the most effective rat poison in every nook and corner of the depot, but it made no difference. Just as human beings get addicted to pleasant poisons, the rats in the depot also became used to the poison thrown here and there by the manager to kill them, so much so that they started demanding a higher and higher dose of it every day. In case the daily dose was not increased sufficiently, they would all kick up a row, as if fully determined to demolish the godowns.

The manager collected a number of best hunting cats and let them loose in the depot. Unfortunately, the next day, only some remnants of cats' fur and a few odd bones could be found here and there. Apparently, the cats lost the battle against the rats, just like the most deadly poison had.

The manager then started building traps in the depot. There were odd rats that did land up in these traps, but if five of them were caught at night, twenty more were added to their population next day, as breeding was much faster.

At last, as a result of constant deliberations, the manager found a way out. He got three huge cages made of iron. Rats caught alive in the traps were thrown into these cages. After some time, every cage became full of trapped rats. The manager did not feed the rats assembled in the cages. After remaining hungry inside the cages for a few days, these rats assaulted the weakest amongst them, devouring them to satiate their hunger. In this way, as the days went by, the number of rats in the three cages started decreasing. Only the strongest survived, the weaker and the smaller being shredded to serve as fodder for the rest.

The cages that were once full of rats, soon turned into live battle-fields. In the end, only three to four rats were left in each cage. Now the survivors did not wait for hunger to overtake them before attacking their cage-mates. They started preemptive assaults, to get at the neck of others before the others could pounce upon theirs. They would remain on the look-out for a fellow rat going to sleep, or just dozing off, or even losing his alert for a while, and would nab him for turning him into a meal. There were cases when three or four of them joined hands against one another. But in the end, these "allies" would also remain on the watch for an opportune moment to eat up one another.

At last, only one survivor was left in each cage. This was the biggest, the fastest, the cleverest and the most powerful.

When only one rat was left in each cage, the competent manager opened the doors of these cages and let the survivors dash into the depot, one by one.

Addicted to eating their own fellow-creatures, the three well-fed, well-built rapacious rats rushed into the depot the moment the doors of their cages were raised, and they started attacking, strangling and tearing into pieces every single rat they came across in the depot. They ate the ones they could, but killed the rest as a measure of security for fear of being attacked by them if they were left alive.

In this way, the depot that was there at the aforesaid place and time got rid of the rats, at least for some time.

Although the story ends here, I have to ask you a question: How did the competent manager think of a trick like this, which the devil himself could never have thought of? How did he know that the rats would eat up one another?

Let me answer it for you. That rat of a competent manager was himself the most powerful survivor who had killed his own fellow creatures one by one, having fed himself upon his own friends, and ultimately managing to become the chief of the huge depot. He made use of the success of his own life, applying it to the rats in the depot.

The moral of the story is: Rats eat one another.

The New Prime Minister

Once upon a time, in one of the countries of this world, there was a king. Like all kings, this particular king had his own set of musicians, dancers, concubines, slaves, boot lickers, and so on. Similarly, like kings of all other countries, this king was also very fond of hunting. Whenever he could steal some time from his multifarious official activities like performing opening ceremonies, taking salutes at ceremonial parades and march pasts, reading out speeches written by others and undertaking tours, he would go on hunting trips.

Being very susceptible to humidity in the air, the king never went hunting without ascertaining the weather conditions he was going to meet during such missions. He would call his chief astrologer and get a weather forecast from him. The chief astrologer would always reply as follows:

"Long live your Exalted Majesty, because of whom the weather of our country always remains bright and full of sunshine. The weather is going to remain as good as your Majesty would like it to be."

Being highly suspicious like all kings, our king would call his prime minister and ask him what the weather was going to be. The mighty prime minister, the very bristles of whose ears had also turned grey and who had a long beard that reached the lower edge of his tummy, would kneel till his beard touched the king's feet, and would then say:

"Under your Majesty's benign shadow, the weather inside the country as well as outside, both political and non-political, is going to be very fine."

The suspicious king would then ask each of his ministers in turn about the weather and get a reply which ran something like this:

"The horizon is pink and the weather is bright. May God always let your Majesty's benign shadow protect our heads, for so long as your Majesty is there, there can be no possibility of the weather being anything other than good."

Finally, relying on his own self-confidence and tremendous power, and keeping in view the considered advice of his experts and political leaders, the king would set out for the special forest where specially reared animals would be waiting for him to find a good game. His hunting gear would be loaded on the backs of specially selected men. He would plonk himself in the middle of a large caravan, with the police and the gendarme in front, protective detachments from the army on the flanks, plus hordes of volunteers scattered all along the route, each one of them ready to sacrifice his life for the monarch. In addition, a large contingent of civil and military officials accompanied the king on such expeditions.

Things were proceeding quite smoothly when, one day, the king was pleased to express his desire to go hunting the next day. He enquired from the chief astrologer, the prime minister, each of his cabinet ministers, the Shaikh-ul Islam, the Secretary-general, the Agha in charge of concubines, the court chamberlain, and so on down the line in accordance with the rank and status of the individuals concerned, as to how the weather was going to be. Having got the usual answer from everybody, he set out on the hunting expedition in the usual manner.

Although all the routes on which the royal caravan was going to pass had been thoroughly combed by the security staff, and every commoner had been kept away from the royal route, a villager with his donkey somehow managed to stay on under the shade of a tree along the road. It so happened that the king had never seen a villager in his life. Seeing a bare-footed creature wrapped in rags, he started wondering what it was. He could never imagine that it could be anything other than an inanimate object. He proceeded towards the villager to satisfy his curiosity. When he was convinced that the quaint object confronting him was a living being, the king asked him in surprise:

"Who are you? A human being or a jinn?"

"I am not a jinn," replied the villager. "I am as much the son of Adam as you are."

On hearing such a rude reply, the king became furious. He thundered:

"What insolence! Such stuff can never be from the same species as I am. Hurry up and let his head roll off his neck."

Before the scimitar of the chief executioner landed on the thin-as-a-bristle neck of the villager, the king shouted:

"Hold on!" And then addressing the villager, he spoke thus:

"O strange creature, whose words do resemble human speech, I want to ask you something. If you can give me the answer, your neck shall be spared. Can you tell me how the weather is going to behave today?"

"A few minutes from now, strong winds will start blowing. Then there will be torrential rain, accompanied by a severe storm," replied the villager.

Infuriated on hearing these words of the villager, the king exploded:

"O you traitor of a man! Don't you know if I make up my mind to go hunting, it is just not possible for the weather to go bad? How can it rain when My Majesty is out for gaming? Come on folks, tie this creature to the tail of a mule immediately!"

They tied the villager to the tail of his own donkey which, in turn, was tied to the tail of a mule. The royal party then moved off to the reserved forest, singing and shouting. They had hardly covered the distance of an arrow throw when the sky became overcast. Thick dark clouds started hovering and the royal caravan was soon overtaken by strong lightning and a thunder storm. Then it started raining so heavily that the whole area was flooded in no time. Strong winds howled ferociously, lashing everything that came their way. The king got away from this mess with great difficulty. He was so angry that the moment he reached the royal palace, he fired all those who had provided him misleading information about the weather. This included the chief astrologer, the prime minister, all the cabinet ministers, and every official of the court concerned with the weather forecast. A few heads were also made to roll. Such was the fury of the king.

The king now called the villager whose forecast about the inclement weather had turned out to be true. Having been dragged for a long distance, tied to the donkey's tail, the poor soul looked completely exhausted. The king bestowed upon him the seal of the Prime Minister and said:

"I hereby declare you to be the country's Prime Minister with immediate effect."

The villager had hardly worked as the country's new Prime Minister for a few days when the king, having by now regained his senses, called him to his court and said:

"Tell me, how did you know that day that it was going to rain?"

"Your Majesty," replied the Prime Minister, "I keep a watch on my donkey's ears and that helps me predict the weather accurately. If there are chances of rain, my donkey's ears which normally remain erect, assume a drooping position. That day, I saw his ears in this position and therefore told you that it was going to rain."

"What thoughtlessness on my part!" mused the king. "It wasn't this villager who predicted the weather accurately; it was actually his donkey who did that. And here we have a whole lot of ministers and a mighty Prime Minister who do not know what even a donkey knows. I think I have deprived the donkey of his right to be this country's Prime Minister, by giving the Prime Minister's seal to this villager."

Without the loss of another moment, the king fired the villager and appointed the ass as his new Prime Minister. Thereafter, whenever the weather was likely to be good, the new Prime Minister would start braying with joy and the king would get the message. In case a storm was approaching, the Prime Minister would raise his tail, and in case it was going to rain, his ears would at once assume a drooping position.

The king lived happily thereafter. He never ignored the advice of his new Prime Minister, particularly whenever he wished to go out hunting.